Lectionary
Advent 2022 to the eve of Advent 2023 (Year A)

Church House Publishing

Published by	Church House Publishing
	Church House
	Great Smith Street
	London SW1P 3AZ

Compilation ©   *The Archbishops' Council 2022*

ISBN   978-0-7151-2393-5 (standard)
978-0-7151-2403-1 (large)
978-0-7151-2394-2 (Kindle edition)
978-0-7151-2395-9 (Core Source ePub)

All rights reserved   No part of this publication may be reproduced in any form or by
any means, electronic or mechanical, including photocopying,
recording, or any information storage and retrieval system, except
as stated below, without written permission which should be
sought from the Copyright Administrator, The Archbishops'
Council, Church House, Great Smith Street, London SW1P 3AZ
Email: copyright@churchofengland.org

Authorization   The Common Worship Calendar and Lectionaries are authorized
pursuant to Canon B 2 of the Canons of the Church of England for
use until further resolution of the General Synod of the Church of
England.

Copyright and Acknowledgements   The Revised Common Lectionary is copyright © The Consultation on
Common Texts: 1992. The Church of England adaptations to the
Principal Service Lectionary are copyright © The Archbishops'
Council, as are the Second and Third Service Lectionaries, the
Weekday Lectionary for Morning and Evening Prayer and the
Additional Weekday Lectionary.

The Daily Eucharistic Lectionary derives, with some adaptation,
from the Ordo Lectionum Missae of the Roman Catholic Church
and is reproduced by permission of The International Commission
on English in the Liturgy.

Edited by Peter Moger
Designed by Derek Birdsall & John Morgan/Omnific
Typeset by RefineCatch Ltd, Bungay, Suffolk
Printed in England by Core Publications Ltd

Contents of this booklet

This booklet gives details of the full range of possibilities envisaged in the liturgical calendar and lectionary of Common Worship. Its use as a tool for the preparation of worship will require the making of several choices based first on the general celebration of the Christian year by the Church of England as a whole; second on the customary pattern of calendar in the diocese, parish and place of worship; and third on the pattern of services locally.

The **first column** comprises the Calendar of the Church with the days of the year. Observances that are mandatory are printed either in **bold** type (Sundays), in **bold** type (Principal Feasts and Holy Days) or in roman (Festivals). Optional celebrations (Lesser Festivals) and Commemorations are printed in ordinary roman type and *italic* type respectively.

The **second column** comprises (a) the readings and psalms for the Principal Service on Sundays, Principal Feasts and Holy Days, and Festivals, and (b) Holy Communion readings and psalms for other days of the week. On the Sundays after Trinity, the Old Testament reading and its psalm are divided into two smaller columns, indicating a choice between a 'continuous' reading week by week or a reading 'related' to the Gospel for that day.

The **third column** comprises (a) the Third Service readings and psalms for Sundays, Principal Feasts and Holy Days, and Festivals, and (b) the readings and psalms for weekday Morning Prayer.

The **fourth column** comprises (a) the Second Service readings and psalms for Sundays, Principal Feasts and Holy Days, and Festivals, and (b) the readings and psalms for weekday Evening Prayer.

An **Additional Weekday Lectionary**, intended particularly for use in places of worship that attract occasional rather than daily worshippers, is provided on pages 75–83. It may be used either at Morning or Evening Prayer.

Common of the Saints

General readings and psalms for saints' days can be found on pages 85–89; for some particular celebrations, other readings are suggested there.

Special Occasions

Readings and psalms for special occasions can be found on pages 90–91.

Liturgical colours

Appropriate liturgical colours are suggested in this booklet. They are not mandatory; traditional or local use may be followed.

Colours are indicated by single letters: the first (always upper case) for the season or Festival; and occasionally a second (lower case) for an optional celebration on that day. Thus, for example, *Gr* for the celebration of a Lesser Festival whose liturgical colour is red, in an otherwise 'green' season.

The following abbreviations are used:

G	Green
P or p	Purple or Violet
P(La)	Purple or Lent array
R or r	Red
W or w	White (Gold is indicated where its use would be appropriate)

Notes on the Lectionary

Sundays, Principal Feasts and Holy Days and Festivals

Three sets of psalms and readings are provided for each Sunday, Principal Feast or Holy Day and Festival.

The **Principal Service lectionary** (based on the Revised Common Lectionary) is intended for use at the principal service of the day (whether this service is Holy Communion or some other authorized form). In most Church communities, this is likely to be the mid-morning service, but the minister is free to decide which service time normally constitutes the Principal Service of the day. This lectionary may be used twice if required – for example, at an early celebration of Holy Communion and then again at a later one.

If only **two readings** are used at the Principal Service and that service is Holy Communion, the second reading must always be the Gospel reading. When the Principal Service lectionary is used at a service other than Holy Communion, the Gospel reading need not always be chosen.

The **Second Service lectionary** is intended for a second main service. In many churches, this lectionary may be the appropriate provision for a Sunday afternoon or evening service. A Gospel reading is always provided so that this lectionary can, if necessary, be used where the second main service is a celebration of Holy Communion.

The **Third Service lectionary**, with shorter readings, is intended where a third set of psalms and readings is needed and is most appropriate for use at an office. A Gospel reading is not always provided, so this lectionary is not suitable for use at Holy Communion.

Weekdays

The Common Worship Weekday Lectionary authorized by the General Synod in 2005 comprises a lectionary (with psalms) for Holy Communion, a lectionary for Morning and Evening Prayer, and tables of psalms for Morning and Evening Prayer.

The **Daily Eucharistic Lectionary** (based on the Roman Catholic daily eucharistic lectionary) is a semi-continuous two-year lectionary with a wide use of scripture, though not complete coverage of the Bible. Two readings are provided for each day, the first from either the Old or New Testament, the second always a Gospel. Psalm provision is intended to be a brief response to the first reading. It is for use at Holy Communion normally in places with a daily or near-daily celebration with a regular congregation. It may also be used as an office lectionary.

The **lectionary for Morning and Evening Prayer** always provides two readings for each office, the first from the Old Testament and the second from the New Testament. These are generally in sequence. One of the New Testament readings for any particular day is from the Gospels.

The **psalms for Morning and Evening Prayer** follow a sequential pattern in Ordinary Time (apart from the period from All Saints to the beginning of Advent).

In the periods from All Saints until 18 December, from the Epiphany until the Presentation of Christ in the Temple (Candlemas), from Ash Wednesday until Palm Sunday, and from the Monday after Easter Week until Pentecost, there is a choice of psalms at Morning and Evening Prayer. The psalms printed first reflect the theme of the season. Alternatively, the psalms from the Ordinary Time cycle may be used. The two sets are separated by 'or'.

From 19 December until the Epiphany and from the Monday of Holy Week until the Saturday of Easter Week, only seasonal psalms are provided.

Where more than one psalm is given, one psalm (printed in **bold**) may be used as the sole psalm at that office.

Guidance on how these options for saying the psalms are expressed typographically can be found in the 'Notes on the Lectionary' below.

A further cycle is provided (see table on page 92), which is largely the monthly sequential cycle of psalms given in the Book of Common Prayer.

A single psalm for use by those who say only one office each day is provided in Prayer During the Day in Common Worship: Daily Prayer.

An **Additional Weekday Lectionary**, intended particularly for use in places of worship that attract occasional rather than daily worshippers, is provided on pages 75–83. It can be used either at Morning or Evening Prayer. Psalmody is not provided and should be taken from provision outlined above.

Using the Lectionary tables

All **Bible references** (except to the Psalms) are to the *New Revised Standard Version* (New York, 1989). Those who use other Bible translations should check the verse numbers against the *NRSV*. Each reference gives book, chapter and verse, in that order.

References to the Psalms are to the Common Worship psalter, published in *Common Worship: Services and Prayers for the Church of England* (2000) and *Common Worship: Daily Prayer* (2005). A table showing the verse number differences between this and the psalter in the *Book of Common Prayer* is provided on the Church of England website (https://www.churchofengland.org/prayer-and-worship/worship-texts-and-resources/common-worship/daily-prayer/psalter/psalter-verse).

Options in the provision of readings or psalms are presented in the following ways:
¶ square brackets [xx] give either optional additional verses or Psalms, or a shorter alternative;
¶ `or' indicates a simple choice between two alternative readings or courses of psalms;
¶ a psalm printed in **bold** may be used as the sole psalm at that office;
¶ on weekdays a psalm printed in parentheses (xx) is omitted if it has been used as the opening canticle at that office;
¶ a psalm marked with an asterisk may be shortened if desired.

Where a reading from the **Apocrypha** is offered, an alternative Old Testament reading is provided.

In the choice of **readings other than the Gospel** reading, the minister should ensure that, in any year, a balance is maintained between readings from the Old and New Testaments and that, where a particular biblical book is appointed to be read over several weeks, the choice ensures that the continuity of one book is not lost.

On the Sundays after Trinity, the Principal Service Lectionary provides **alternative Old Testament readings and psalms**. References in the left-hand column (under the heading 'Continuous') offer a *semi-continuous* reading of Old Testament texts. Such a reading and its complementary psalmody stand independently of the other readings. References in the right-hand column (under the heading 'Related') *relate* the Old Testament reading and the psalm to the Gospel reading. One column should be followed for the whole sequence of Sundays after Trinity.

The Lectionary 2022–2023

The Sunday and festal readings for 27 November 2022 (the First Sunday of Advent) to 2 December 2023 (the eve of Advent Sunday) are from **Year A**, which offers a semi-continuous reading of Matthew's Gospel at the Principal Service on Sundays throughout the year.

The weekday readings for Holy Communion are from **Year One** of the Daily Eucharistic Lectionary (DEL).

Office readings are from Table 2 of the Weekday Lectionary (Old Testament 2a and New Testament 2) at Morning Prayer and from Table 1 of the Weekday Lectionary (Old Testament 1 and New Testament 1) at Evening Prayer.

Notes on the Calendar 27 November 2022— 2 December 2023

These notes are based on the Rules to Order the Christian Year (*Common Worship: Times and Seasons*, pages 24–30).

Sundays

All Sundays celebrate the paschal mystery of the death and resurrection of the Lord. They also reflect the character of the seasons in which they are set.

Principal Feasts

On these days (printed in **bold**) Holy Communion is celebrated in every cathedral and in at least one church in each benefice or, where benefices are held in plurality, in at least one church in at least one of those benefices, and this celebration, required by Canon B 14, may not be displaced by any other celebration, and may be dispensed with only in accordance with the provision of Canon B 14A.

Except in the case of Christmas Day and Easter Day, the celebration of the Feast *begins with Evening Prayer on the day before the Feast*, and the Collect at that Evening Prayer is that of the Feast. In the case of Christmas Eve and Easter Eve, there is proper liturgical provision (including a Collect) for the whole day.

The Epiphany may, for pastoral reasons, be celebrated on Sunday 8 January. **The Presentation** may, for pastoral reasons, be celebrated on Sunday 29 January. **All Saints' Day** may, for pastoral reasons, be celebrated on Sunday 5 November. If so, there may be a supplementary celebration on Wednesday 1 November.

Other Principal Holy Days

These days (printed in **bold**), and the liturgical provision for them, may not be displaced by any other celebration.

Ash Wednesday (22 February) and **Maundy Thursday** (6 April) are Principal Holy Days. On both these days Holy Communion is celebrated in every cathedral and in at least one church in each benefice or, where benefices are held in plurality, in at least one church in at least one of those benefices, except where there is dispensation under Canon B 14A.

Good Friday (7 April) is a Principal Holy Day.

Eastertide

The paschal character of **the Great Fifty Days of Easter**, from Easter Day (9 April) to Pentecost (28 May), should be celebrated throughout the season, and should not be displaced by other celebrations. No Festival day may be celebrated in Easter Week; and nor may any Festival – except for a Patronal or Dedication Festival – displace the celebration of a Sunday (a memorial of the resurrection) during Eastertide. The paschal character of the season should be retained on those weekdays when saints' days are celebrated.

The three days before Ascension Day (15–17 May) are customarily observed as **Rogation Days**, when prayer is offered for God's blessing on the fruits of the earth and on human labour.

The nine days **after Ascension Day until the eve of Pentecost** (19–27 May) are observed as days of prayer and preparation for the celebration of the outpouring of the Holy Spirit.

Ordinary Time

Ordinary Time comprises two periods in the year: first, the period from the day after the Presentation of Christ in the Temple until the day before Ash Wednesday, and second, that from the day after Pentecost until the day before the First Sunday of Advent.

During Ordinary Time, there is no seasonal emphasis, except that the period between All Saints' Day and the First Sunday of Advent is a time to celebrate and reflect upon the reign of Christ in earth and heaven.

Festivals

These days (printed in roman), and the liturgical provision for them, are not usually displaced. For each day there is full liturgical provision for a Principal, Second and Third Service, and an optional so-called First Evening Prayer on the evening before the Festival where this is required.

Festivals may *not* be celebrated on Sundays in Advent, Lent or Eastertide, the Baptism of Christ, Ascension Day, Trinity Sunday or Christ the King, or on weekdays between Palm Sunday and the Second Sunday of Easter.

Otherwise, a Festival falling on a Sunday – namely in 2022–23, the Naming and Circumcision of Jesus (falling on the Second Sunday of Christmas), Barnabas the Apostle (falling on the First Sunday after Trinity), and the Transfiguration of Our Lord (falling on the Ninth Sunday after Trinity) – may be kept on that Sunday or transferred: the Naming and Circumcision to Monday 2 January, Barnabas to Monday 12 June, and the Transfiguration to Monday 7 August (or, at the discretion of the minister, to the next suitable weekday).

Certain Festivals (namely, Matthias the Apostle, the Visit of the BVM to Elizabeth, Thomas the Apostle, and the Blessed Virgin Mary) have customary alternative dates (see p.8).

The Thursday after Trinity Sunday (8 June) may be observed as the **Day of Thanksgiving for the Institution of Holy Communion** (sometimes known as *Corpus Christi*), and may be kept as a Festival.

Other Celebrations

Mothering Sunday falls on the Fourth Sunday of Lent (19 March). Alternative prayers and readings are provided for the Principal Service. **Bible Sunday** may be celebrated on 29 October, replacing the Last Sunday after Trinity, and appropriate prayers and readings are provided.

Local Celebrations

The celebration of **the patron saint or the title of a church** is kept either as a Festival or as a Principal Feast.

The **Dedication Festival** of a church is the anniversary of the date of its dedication or consecration. This is kept either as a Festival or as a Principal Feast. When kept as Principal Feasts, the Patronal and Dedication Festivals may be transferred to the nearest Sunday, unless that day is already a Principal Feast or one of the following days: the First Sunday of Advent, the Baptism of Christ, the First Sunday of Lent, the Fifth Sunday of Lent, or Palm Sunday. If the actual date is not known, the Dedication Festival may be celebrated on 1 October (replacing the Seventeenth Sunday after Trinity), or on 29 October (replacing the Last Sunday after Trinity), or on a suitable date chosen locally. Readings can be found on page 84.

Harvest Thanksgiving may be celebrated on any Sunday in autumn, replacing the provision for that day, provided it does not displace any Principal Feast or Festival.

Diocesan and other local provision may be made in **the calendar of the saints** to supplement the general calendar, in accordance with Canon B 6, paragraph 5.

Lesser Festivals

Lesser Festivals (printed in ordinary roman type, in black) are observed in a manner appropriate to a particular place. Each is provided with a Collect, which may supersede the Collect of the week. For certain Lesser Festivals a complete set of Eucharistic readings is provided, and for others appropriate readings may be selected from the Common of the Saints (see pages 85–89). These readings may, at the minister's discretion, supersede the Daily Eucharistic Lectionary (DEL). The weekday psalms and readings at Morning and Evening Prayer are not usually superseded by those for Lesser Festivals, but at the minister's discretion psalms and readings provided on these days for use at Holy Communion may be used instead at Morning or Evening Prayer.

The minister may be selective in the Lesser Festivals that are observed and may also keep some, or all of them, as Commemorations, perhaps especially in Advent, Lent and Easter where the character of the season ought to be sustained. If the Day of Thanksgiving for the Institution of Holy Communion (8 June) is not kept as a Festival in 2023, it may be kept as a Lesser Festival.

When a Lesser Festival falls on a Principal Feast or Holy Day, a Festival, a Sunday, or on a weekday between Palm Sunday and the Second Sunday of Easter, its celebration is normally omitted for that year. However, where there is sufficient reason, it may, at the discretion of the minister, be celebrated on the nearest available day.

Commemorations

Commemorations (printed in *italic*) are made by a mention in prayers of intercession. They are not provided with Collect, Psalm and Readings, and do not replace the usual weekday provision at Holy Communion or at Morning and Evening Prayer.

The minister may be selective in the Commemorations that are made.

Only where there is an established celebration in the wider Church or where the day has a special local significance may a Commemoration be observed as a Lesser Festival, with liturgical provision from the Common of the Saints (pages 85–89).

In designating a Commemoration as a Lesser Festival, the minister must remember the need to maintain the spirit of the season, especially of Advent, Lent and Easter.

Days of Discipline and Self-Denial

The weekdays of Lent and every Friday in the year are days of discipline and self-denial, with the exception of Principal Feasts, Festivals outside Lent, and Fridays from Easter Day to Pentecost. The day preceding a Principal Feast may also be appropriately kept as a day of discipline and self-denial in preparation for the Feast.

Ember Days

Ember Days should be kept, under the bishop's directions, in the week before an ordination as days of prayer for those to be ordained deacon or priest.

Ember Days may also be kept even when there is no ordination in the diocese as more general days of prayer for those who serve the Church in its various ministries, both ordained and lay, and for vocations. Traditionally they have been observed on the Wednesday, Friday and Saturday in the week before the Third Sunday of Advent, the Second Sunday of Lent, and the Sundays nearest to 29 June and 29 September.

Notes on Collects

For a table showing where the Collects and Post Communions are published, see page 84.

Where a Collect ends 'through Jesus Christ ... now and for ever', the minister may omit the longer (trinitarian) ending and use the shorter ending, 'through Jesus Christ our Lord', to which the people respond, 'Amen'. The longer ending, however, is to be preferred at a service of Holy Communion.

The Collect for each Sunday is used at Evening Prayer on the Saturday preceding, except where that Saturday is a Principal Feast, or a Festival, or the eve of Christmas Day or Easter Day. The Collect for each Sunday is also used on the weekdays following, except where other provision is made.

Abbreviations used in this book

Alt	Alternative
BVM	Blessed Virgin Mary
DEL	Daily Eucharistic Lectionary
EP	Evening Prayer
G	Green

HC	Holy Communion: used where *additional references are given to provide alternative texts for use at a celebration of Holy Communion (most often the provision of a psalm or gospel)*
MP	Morning Prayer

P or p	Purple or Violet
P(La)	Purple or Lent Array
Ps & Pss	Psalmody
R or r	Red
W or w	White (Gold is indicated where its use would be appropriate)

Alternative dates

The following may be celebrated on the alternative dates indicated:

Thomas Becket
– on 7 July 2023 instead of 29 December 2022

Chad
– with Cedd on 26 October instead of 2 March

Cuthbert
– on 4 September instead of 20 March

Thomas the Apostle
– on 21 December 2022 instead of 3 July 2023

Matthias the Apostle
– on 24 February instead of 15 May (transferred from 14 May)

The Visit of the Blessed Virgin Mary to Elizabeth
– on 2 July or transferred to 3 July (if Thomas the Apostle is celebrated on 21 December 2022) or 4 July instead of 31 May

The Blessed Virgin Mary
– on 8 September instead of 15 August

If any of the four festivals is celebrated on the alternative date these provisions should be used on the principal date:

Holy Communion	Morning Prayer	Evening Prayer
If Thomas the Apostle is celebrated on Wednesday 21 December 2022, the following provision is used on Monday 3 July 2023 (G):		
Genesis 18.16–end	Psalms **80**, 82	Psalms **85**, 86
Psalm 103.6–17	Nehemiah 4	Judges 13.1–24
Matthew 8.18–22	Romans 14.13–end	Luke 17.20–end
If Matthias the Apostle is celebrated on Friday 24 February, the following provision is used on Monday 15 May (W):		
Acts 16.11–15	Psalms **65**, 67 or **80**, 82	Psalms **121**, 122, 123 or **85**, 86
Psalm 149.1–5	Deuteronomy 26	Numbers 16.1–35
John 15.26—16.4	1 Peter 4.1–11	Luke 6.27–38
If the Visit of the Blessed Virgin Mary to Elizabeth is celebrated on 2, 3 or 4 July, the following provision is used on Wednesday 31 May (G):		
Ecclesiasticus 36.1–2, 4–5, 10–17	Psalm 119.**153**–end	Psalm **136**
or James 4.13–end	2 Chronicles 18.2—end of 19	Joshua 3
Psalm 79.8–9, 12, 14 or 49.1–2, 5–10	Romans 2.1–16	Luke 9.37–50
Mark 10.32–45		
If the Blessed Virgin Mary is celebrated on Friday 8 September, the following provision is used on Tuesday 15 August (G):		
Deuteronomy 31.1–8	Psalm **73**	Psalm **74**
Psalm 107.1–3, 42–end	Jeremiah 42	1 Samuel 26
or Canticle: Deuteronomy 32.3–4, 7–9	Mark 3.7–19a	Acts 4.1–12
Matthew 18.1–5, 10, 12–14		

8

For guidance on how the options for saying the psalms are expressed typographically, see page 5.

Sundays (and Principal Feasts, other Principal Holy Days, and Festivals)

		Principal Service	3rd Service	2nd Service
Day	**Date** Sunday / Feast † / Festival ††	**Colour**	Main service of the day: **Holy Communion, Morning Prayer, Evening Prayer, or a Service of the Word**	Shorter Readings, an Office lectionary probably used at Morning Prayer where Holy Communion is the Principal Service	2nd main service, probably used at Evening Prayer; adaptable for Holy Communion

† Principal Feasts and other Principal Holy Days are printed in **bold**.
†† Festivals are printed in roman typeface.

Weekdays

		Holy Communion	Morning Prayer	Evening Prayer
Day	**Date**	Colour	Weekday readings	Psalms and readings for Morning Prayer	Psalms and readings for Evening Prayer

Lesser Festival ‡* [optional]
Commemoration ‡‡ [optional]

‡ Lesser Festivals are printed in roman typeface, in black.
‡‡ Commemorations are printed in *italics*.
* The ascriptions given to holy men and women in the Calendar (such as martyr, teacher of the faith, etc.) have often been abbreviated in this booklet for reasons of space.
The particular ascription given is there to be helpful if needing to choose Collects and readings from Common of the Saints; where several ascriptions are used (e.g. bishop and martyr), traditionally the last ascription given is the most important and therefore the guiding one. The full ascriptions may be found in the Calendar, which is printed in *Common Worship: Times and Seasons* (pages 7–22), *Common Worship: Festivals* (pages 5–20) and *Common Worship: Daily Prayer* (pages 5–16). These incorporate minor corrections made since the publication of the Calendar in *Common Worship: Services and Prayers for the Church of England* (pages 5–16).

		Principal Service	3rd Service	2nd Service
Sunday	**27 November** P **1st Sunday of Advent**	Isaiah 2.1-5 Psalm 122 Romans 13.11-end Matthew 24.36-44	Psalm 44 Micah 4.1-7 1 Thessalonians 5.1-11	Psalm 9 [or 9.1-8] Isaiah 52.1-12 Matthew 24.15-28
		Holy Communion	**Morning Prayer**	**Evening Prayer**
Monday	**28 November** P	Isaiah 4.2-end Psalm 122 Matthew 8.5-11	Psalms 50, 54 or 1, 2, 3 Isaiah 42.18-end Revelation 19	Psalms 70, 71 or 4, 7 Isaiah 25.1-9 Matthew 12.1-21
Tuesday	**29 November** P *Day of Intercession and Thanksgiving for the* *Missionary Work of the Church*	Isaiah 11.1-10 Psalm 72.1-4, 18-19 Luke 10.21-24	Psalms 80, 82 or 5, 6 (8) Isaiah 43.1-13 Revelation 20	Psalms 74, 75 or 9, 10* Isaiah 26.1-13 Matthew 12.22-37 *or:* 1st EP of Andrew the Apostle: Psalm 48; Isaiah 49.1-9a; 1 Corinthians 4.9-16
		Principal Service	**3rd Service**	**2nd Service**
Wednesday	**30 November** R Andrew the Apostle	Isaiah 52.7-10 Psalm 19.1-6 Romans 10.12-18 Matthew 4.18-22	MP Psalms 47, 147.1-12 Ezekiel 47.1-12 or Ecclesiasticus 14.20-end John 12.20-32	EP Psalms 87, 96 Zechariah 8.20-end John 1.35-42
		Holy Communion	**Morning Prayer**	**Evening Prayer**
Thursday	**1 December** P *Charles de Foucauld, hermit, 1916*	Isaiah 26.1-6 Psalm 118.18-27a Matthew 7.21, 24-27	Psalms 42, 43 or 14, 15, 16 Isaiah 44.1-8 Revelation 21.9-21	Psalms 40, 46 or 18* Isaiah 28.14-end Matthew 13.1-23
Friday	**2 December** P	Isaiah 29.17-end Psalm 27.1-4, 16-17 Matthew 9.27-31	Psalms 25, 26 or 17, 19 Isaiah 44.9-23 Revelation 21.22—22.5	Psalms 16, 17 or 22 Isaiah 29.1-14 Matthew 13.24-43
Saturday	**3 December** P *Francis Xavier, missionary, 1552*	Isaiah 30.19-21, 23-26 Psalm 146.4-9 Matthew 9.35—10.1, 6-8	Psalms 9, (10) or 20, 21, 23 Isaiah 44.24—45.13 Revelation 22.6-end	Psalms 27, 28 or 24, 25 Isaiah 29.15-end Matthew 13.44-end

		Principal Service	3rd Service	2nd Service
		Holy Communion	Morning Prayer	Evening Prayer
Sunday	**4 December** P **2nd Sunday of Advent**	Isaiah 11.1–10 Psalm 72.1–7, 18–19 [or 72.1–7] Romans 15.4–13 Matthew 3.1–12	Psalm 80 Amos 7 Luke 1.5–20	Psalms 11 [28] 1 Kings 18.17–39 John 1.19–28
Monday	**5 December** P	Isaiah 35 Psalm 85.7–end Luke 5.17–26	Psalm 44 or 27, **30** Isaiah 45.14–end 1 Thessalonians 1	Psalms 144, 146 or 26, **28**, 29 Isaiah 30.1–18 Matthew 14.1–12
Tuesday	**6 December** Pw Nicholas, bishop, c.326 (see p.87)	Isaiah 40.1–11 Psalm 96.1, 10–end Matthew 18.12–14	Psalms **56**, 57 or 32, **36** Isaiah 46 1 Thessalonians 2.1–12	Psalms 11, 12, 13 or **33** Isaiah 30.19–end Matthew 14.13–end
Wednesday	**7 December** Pw Ambrose, bishop, teacher of the faith, 397 (see p.86) Ember Day	Isaiah 40.25–end Psalm 103.8–13 Matthew 11.28–end	Psalms 62, 63 or **34** Isaiah 47 1 Thessalonians 2.13–end	Psalms 10, 14 or **119.33–56** Isaiah 31 Matthew 15.1–20
Thursday	**8 December** Pw Conception of the Blessed Virgin Mary (see p.85)	Isaiah 41.13–20 Psalm 145.1, 8–13 Matthew 11.11–15	Psalms 53, **54**, 60 or **37*** Isaiah 48.1–11 1 Thessalonians 3	Psalm **73** or 39, **40** Isaiah 32 Matthew 15.21–28
Friday	**9 December** P Ember Day	Isaiah 48.17–19 Psalm 1 Matthew 11.16–19	Psalms 85, **86** or **31** Isaiah 48.12–end 1 Thessalonians 4.1–12	Psalms 82, **90** or **35** Isaiah 33.1–22 Matthew 15.29–end
Saturday	**10 December** P Ember Day	Ecclesiasticus 48.1–4, 9–11 or 2 Kings 2.9–12 Psalm 80.1–4, 18–19 Matthew 17.10–13	Psalm 145 or 41, **42**, 43 Isaiah 49.1–13 1 Thessalonians 4.13–end	Psalms 93, **94** or 45, **46** Isaiah 35 Matthew 16.1–12

	Principal Service	3rd Service	2nd Service
Sunday *P* **11 December** **3rd Sunday of Advent**	Isaiah 35.1–10 Psalm 146.4–10 or *Canticle:* Magnificat James 5.7–10 Matthew 11.2–11	Psalm 68.1–19 Zephaniah 3.14–end Philippians 4.4–7	Psalms 12 [14] Isaiah 5.8–end Acts 13.13–41 *HC* John 5.31–40
	Holy Communion	**Morning Prayer**	**Evening Prayer**
Monday *P* **12 December**	Numbers 24.2–7, 15–17 Psalm 25.3–8 Matthew 21.23–27	Psalm **40** or **44** Isaiah 49.14–25 1 Thessalonians 5.1–11	Psalms 25, **26** or **47**, 49 Isaiah 38. 1–8, 21–22 Matthew 16.13–end
Tuesday *Pr* **13 December** Lucy, martyr, 304 (see p.85) *Samuel Johnson, moralist, 1784*	Zephaniah 3.1–2, 9–13 Psalm 34.1–6, 21–22 Matthew 21.28–32	Psalm **70**, 74 or **48**, 52 Isaiah 50 1 Thessalonians 5.12–end	Psalms **50**, 54 or **50** Isaiah 38. 9–20 Matthew 17.1–13
Wednesday *Pw* **14 December** John of the Cross, poet, teacher of the faith, 1591 (see p.86)	Isaiah 45.6b–8, 18, 21b–end Psalm 85.7–end Luke 7.18b–23	Psalms **75**, 96 or 119. **57–80** Isaiah 51.1–8 2 Thessalonians 1	Psalms 25, **82** or **59**, 60 (67) Isaiah 39 Matthew 17.14–21
Thursday *P* **15 December**	Isaiah 54.1–10 Psalm 30.1–5, 11–end Luke 7.24–30	Psalms **76**, 97 or 56, **57** (63*) Isaiah 51.9–16 2 Thessalonians 2	Psalm **44** or 61, **62**, 64 Zephaniah 1.1—2.3 Matthew 17.22–end
Friday *P* **16 December**	Isaiah 56.1–3a, 6–8 Psalm 67 John 5.33–36	Psalms 77, **98** or **51**, 54 Isaiah 51.17–end 2 Thessalonians 3	Psalm **49** or **38** Zephaniah 3.1–13 Matthew 18.1–20
Saturday *P* **17 December** *O Sapientia* *Eglantyne Jebb, social reformer,* *founder of 'Save The Children', 1928*	Genesis 49.2, 8–10 Psalm 72.1–5, 18–19 Matthew 1.1–17	Psalm **71** or **68** Isaiah 52.1–12 Jude	Psalms 42, **43** or 65, **66** Zephaniah 3.14–end Matthew 18.21–end

		Principal Service	3rd Service	2nd Service
Sunday	P	Isaiah 7.10–16	Psalm 144	Psalms 113 [126]
18 December		Psalm 80.1–8, 18–20 [or 80.1–8]	Micah 5.2–5a	1 Samuel 1.1–20
4th Sunday of Advent		Romans 1.1–7	Luke 1.26–38	Revelation 22.6–end
		Matthew 1.18–end		HC Luke 1.39–45
		Holy Communion	**Morning Prayer**	**Evening Prayer**
			From Monday 19 December until the Epiphany the seasonal psalmody must be used at Morning and Evening Prayer.	
Monday 19 December	P	Judges 13.2–7, 24–end	Psalms 144, **146**	Psalms 10, **57**
		Psalm 71.3–8	Isaiah 52.13—end of 53	Malachi 1.1, 6–end
		Luke 1.5–25	2 Peter 1.1–15	Matthew 19.1–12
Tuesday 20 December	P	Isaiah 7.10–14	Psalms **46**, 95	Psalms **4**, 9
		Psalm 24.1–6	Isaiah 54	Malachi 2.1–16
		Luke 1.26–38	2 Peter 1.16—2.3	Matthew 19.13–15
Wednesday 21 December	P	Zephaniah 3.14–18	Psalms **121**, 122, 123	Psalms 80, **84**
		Psalm 33.1–4, 11–12, 20–end	Isaiah 55	Malachi 2.17—3.12
		Luke 1.39–45	2 Peter 2.4–end	Matthew 19.16–end
Thursday 22 December	P	1 Samuel 1.24–end	Psalms **124**, 125, 126, 127	Psalms 24, **48**
		Psalm 113	Isaiah 56.1–8	Malachi 3.13—end of 4
		Luke 1.46–56	2 Peter 3	Matthew 23.1–12
Friday 23 December	P	Malachi 3.1–4, 4.5–end	Psalms 128, 129, **130**, 131	Psalm **89.1–37**
		Psalm 25.3–9	Isaiah 63.1–6	Nahum 1
		Luke 1.57–66	2 John	Matthew 23.13–28
Saturday 24 December	P	2 Samuel 7.1–5, 8–11, 16	Psalms **45**, 113	Psalm **85**
Christmas Eve		Psalm 89.2, 19–27	Isaiah 58	Zechariah 2
		Acts 13.16–26	3 John	Revelation 1.1–8
		Luke 1.67–79		

Christmas

	Principal Service	3rd Service	2nd Service
Sunday **25 December** Christmas Day	Gold or W Any of the following three sets of Principal Service readings may be used on the evening of Christmas Eve and on Christmas Day. Set III should be used at some service during the celebration. Set I Isaiah 9.2–7 Psalm 96 Titus 2.11–14 Luke 2.1–14 [15–20] Set II Isaiah 62.6–end Psalm 97 Titus 3.4–7 Luke 2. [1–7] 8–20 Set III Isaiah 52.7–10 Psalm 98 Hebrews 1.1–4 [5–12] John 1.1–14	MP Psalms 110, 117 Isaiah 62.1–5 Matthew 1.18–end	EP Psalm 8 Isaiah 65.17–25 Philippians 2.5–11 or Luke 2.1–20 if it has not been used at the Principal Service of the day
Monday **26 December** Stephen, deacon, first martyr	R 2 Chronicles 24.20–22 or Acts 7.51–end Psalm 119.161–168 Acts 7.51–end or Galatians 2.16b–20 Matthew 10.17–22	MP Psalms 13, 31.1–8, 150 Jeremiah 26.12–15 Acts 6	EP Psalms 57, 86 Genesis 4.1–10 Matthew 23.34–end
Tuesday **27 December** John, Apostle and Evangelist	W Exodus 33.7–11a Psalm 117 1 John 1 John 21.19b–end	MP Psalms 21, 147.13–end Exodus 33.12–end 1 John 2.1–11	EP Psalm 97 Isaiah 6.1–8 1 John 5.1–12
Wednesday **28 December** The Holy Innocents	R Jeremiah 31.15–17 Psalm 124 1 Corinthians 1.26–29 Matthew 2.13–18	MP Psalms 36, 146 Baruch 4.21–27 or Genesis 37.13–20 Matthew 18.1–10	EP Psalms 123, 128 Isaiah 49.14–25 Mark 10.13–16

	Holy Communion	Morning Prayer	Evening Prayer
Thursday **29 December** Thomas Becket, archbishop, martyr, 1170 (see p.85)	Wr 1 John 2.3–11 Psalm 96.1–4 Luke 2.22–35	Psalms 19, 20 Isaiah 57.15–end John 1.1–18	Psalms 131, 132 Jonah 1 Colossians 1.1–14
Friday **30 December**	W 1 John 2.12–17 Psalm 96.7–10 Luke 2.36–40	Psalms 111, 112, 113 Isaiah 59.1–15a John 1.19–28	Psalms 65, 84 Jonah 2 Colossians 1.15–23
Saturday **31 December** John Wyclif, reformer, 1384	W 1 John 2.18–21 Psalm 96.1, 11–end John 1.1–18	Psalm 102 Isaiah 59.15b–end John 1.29–34	Psalms 90, 148 Jonah 3–4 Colossians 1.24–2.7 or: 1st EP of the Naming and Circumcision of Jesus: Psalm 148; Jeremiah 23.1–6; Colossians 2.8–15

If The Naming and Circumcision of Jesus *is celebrated on Sunday 1 January:*

		Principal Service	3rd Service	2nd Service
Sunday	**1 January** W Naming and Circumcision of Jesus	Numbers 6.22–end Psalm 8 Galatians 4.4–7 Luke 2.15–21	*MP* Psalms **103**, 150 Genesis 17.1–13 Romans 2.17–end	*EP* Psalm **115** Deuteronomy 30. [1–10] 11–end Acts 3.1–16
		Holy Communion	**Morning Prayer**	**Evening Prayer**
Monday	**2 January** W Basil the Great and Gregory of Nazianzus, bishops, teachers of the faith, 379 and 389 (see p.86) *Seraphim, monk, spiritual guide, 1833* *Vedanayagam Samuel Azariah, bishop, evangelist, 1945*	1 John 2.22–28 Psalm 98.1–4 John 1.19–28	Psalm **18.1–30** Isaiah 60.1–12 John 1.35–42	Psalms 45, **46** Ruth 1 Colossians 2.8–end

If The Naming and Circumcision of Jesus *is transferred to Monday 2 January:*

		Principal Service	3rd Service	2nd Service
Sunday	**1 January** W **2nd Sunday of Christmas**	Isaiah 63.7–9 Psalm 148 [or 148.7–end] Hebrews 2.10–end Matthew 2.13–end	Psalm 105.1–11 Isaiah 35.1–6 Galatians 3.23–end	Psalm 132 Isaiah 49.7–13 Philippians 2.1–11 *HC* Luke 2.41–52 *or:* 1st EP of the Naming and Circumcision of Jesus: Psalm 148; Jeremiah 23.1–6; Colossians 2.8–15
Monday	**2 January** W Naming and Circumcision of Jesus	Numbers 6.22–end Psalm 8 Galatians 4.4–7 Luke 2.15–21	*MP* Psalms **103**, 150 Genesis 17.1–13 Romans 2.17–end	*EP* Psalm **115** Deuteronomy 30. [1–10] 11–end Acts 3.1–16

Epiphany / Baptism of Christ

If the Epiphany is celebrated on Friday 6 January:

		Holy Communion	Morning Prayer	Evening Prayer
Tuesday 3 January	W	1 John 2.29—3.6 Psalm 98.2-7 John 1.29-34	Psalms **127**, 128, 131 Isaiah 60.13-end John 1.43-end	Psalms **2**, 110 Ruth 2 Colossians 3.1-11
Wednesday 4 January	W	1 John 3.7-10 Psalm 98.1, 8-end John 1.35-42	Psalm **89**.1-37 Isaiah 61 John 2.1-11	Psalms 85, **87** Ruth 3 Colossians 3.12—4.1
Thursday 5 January	W	1 John 3.11-21 Psalm 100 John 1.43-end	Psalms 8, **48** Isaiah 62 John 2.13-end	1st EP of the Epiphany Psalms 96, **97** Isaiah 49.1-13 John 4.7-26
		Principal Service	**3rd Service**	**2nd Service**
Friday 6 January Epiphany	Gold or W	Isaiah 60.1-6 Psalm 72. [1—9] 10-15 Ephesians 3.1-12 Matthew 2.1-12	MP Psalms **132**, 113 Jeremiah 31.7-14 John 1.29-34	EP Psalms **98**, 100 Baruch 4.36—end of 5 or Isaiah 60.1-9 John 2.1-11
		Holy Communion	**Morning Prayer**	**Evening Prayer**
Saturday 7 January	W	1 John 3.22—4.6 Psalm 2.7-end Matthew 4.12-17, 23-end	Psalms 99, 147.1-12 or 76, 79 Isaiah 63.7-end 1 John 3	1st EP of the Baptism of Christ Psalm 36 Isaiah 61 Titus 2.11-14; 3.4-7
		Principal Service	**3rd Service**	**2nd Service**
Sunday 8 January Baptism of Christ 1st Sunday of Epiphany	Gold or W	Isaiah 42.1-9 Psalm 29 Acts 10.34-43 Matthew 3.13-end	Psalm 89.19-29 Exodus 14.15-22 1 John 5.6-9	Psalms 46, 47 Joshua 3.1-8, 14-end Hebrews 1.1-12 HC Luke 3.15-22
		Holy Communion	**Morning Prayer**	**Evening Prayer**
Monday 9 January DEL week 1	W	Hebrews 1.1-6 Psalm 97.1-2, 6-10 Mark 1.14-20	Psalms **2**, 110 or **80**, 82 Amos 1 1 Corinthians 1.1-17	Psalms 34, 36 or **85**, 86 Genesis 1.1-19 Matthew 21.1-17

Epiphany

If the Epiphany is celebrated on Sunday 8 January:

		Holy Communion	Morning Prayer	Evening Prayer
Tuesday 3 January	W	1 John 2.29—3.6 Psalm 98.2–7 John 1.29–34	Psalms **127**, 128, 131 Isaiah 60.13–end John 1.43–end	Psalms **2**, 110 Ruth 2 Colossians 3.1–11
Wednesday 4 January	W	1 John 3.7–10 Psalm 98.1, 8–end John 1.35–42	Psalm **89.1–37** Isaiah 61 John 2.1–12	Psalms 85, **87** Ruth 3 Colossians 3.12—4.1
Thursday 5 January	W	1 John 3.11–21 Psalm 100 John 1.43–end	Psalms 8, **48** Isaiah 62 John 2.13–end	Psalms 96, **97** Ruth 4.1–17 Colossians 4.2–end
Friday 6 January	W	1 John 5.5–13 Psalm 147.13–end Mark 1.7–11	Psalms **46**, 147.13–end Isaiah 63.7–end 1 John 3	Psalm **145** Baruch 1.15—2.10 or Jeremiah 23.1–8 Matthew 20.1–16
Saturday 7 January	W	1 John 5.14–end Psalm 149.1–5 John 2.1–11	Psalms 99, 147.1–12 Isaiah 64 1 John 4.7–end	**1st EP of the Epiphany** Psalms 96, **97** Isaiah 49.1–13 John 4.7–26
		Principal Service	**3rd Service**	**2nd Service**
Sunday 8 January Epiphany	*Gold or* W	Isaiah 60.1–6 Psalm 72. [1–9] 10–15 Ephesians 3.1–12 Matthew 2.1–12	*MP* Psalms **132**, 113 Jeremiah 31.7–14 John 1.29–34	*EP* Psalms **98**, 100 Baruch 4.36–end of 5 or Isaiah 60.1–9 John 2.1–11
Monday 9 January Baptism of Christ	*Gold or* W	Isaiah 42.1–9 Psalm 29 Acts 10.34–43 Matthew 3.13–end	Psalm 89.19–29 Exodus 14.15–22 1 John 5.6–9	Psalms 46, 47 Joshua 3.1–8, 14–end Hebrews 1.1–12 *HC* Luke 3.15–22

17

		Holy Communion	Morning Prayer	Evening Prayer
Tuesday	**10 January** W *William Laud, archbishop, 1645* DEL week 1	Hebrews 2.5–12 Psalm 8 Mark 1.21–28	Psalms 8, 9 or 87, **89**.1–18 Amos 2 1 Corinthians 1.18–end	Psalms **45**, 46 or **89.19–end** Genesis 1.20—2.3 Matthew 21.18–32
Wednesday	**11 January** W *Mary Slessor, missionary, 1915*	Hebrews 2.14–end Psalm 105.1–9 Mark 1.29–39	Psalms 19, **20** or 119.**105–128** Amos 3 1 Corinthians 2	Psalms **47**, 48 or **91**, 93 Genesis 2.4–end Matthew 21.33–end
Thursday	**12 January** W *Aelred, abbot, 1167 (see p.88)* *Benedict Biscop, scholar, 689*	Hebrews 3.7–14 Psalm 95.1, 8–end Mark 1.40–end	Psalms **21**, 24 or 90, **92** Amos 4 1 Corinthians 3	Psalms **61**, 65 or **94** Genesis 3 Matthew 22.1–14
Friday	**13 January** W *Hilary, bishop, teacher of the faith, 367* *(see p.86)* *Kentigern (Mungo), missionary bishop, 603* *George Fox, founder of the* *Society of Friends (Quakers), 1691*	Hebrews 4.1–5 Psalm 78.3–8 Mark 2.1–12	Psalms **67**, 72 or **88** (95) Amos 5.1–17 1 Corinthians 4	Psalm **68** or **102** Genesis 4.1–16, 25–26 Matthew 22.15–33
Saturday	**14 January** W	Hebrews 4.12–end Psalm 19.7–end Mark 2.13–17	Psalms 29, **33** or 96, **97**, 100 Amos 5.18–end 1 Corinthians 5	Psalms 84, **85** or **104** Genesis 6.1–10 Matthew 22.34–end

18

	Principal Service	3rd Service	2nd Service
Sunday **15 January** **2nd Sunday of Epiphany** W	Isaiah 49.1–7 Psalm 40.1–12 1 Corinthians 1.1–9 John 1.29–42	Psalm 145.1–12 Jeremiah 1.4–10 Mark 1.14–20	Psalm 96 Ezekiel 2.1–3.4 Galatians 1.11–end HC John 1.43–end
	Holy Communion	Morning Prayer	Evening Prayer
Monday **16 January** DEL week 2 W	Hebrews 5.1–10 Psalm 110.1–4 Mark 2.18–22	Psalms 145, 146 or 98, 99, 101 Amos 6 1 Corinthians 6.1–11	Psalm 71 or 105* (or 103) Genesis 6.11–7.10 Matthew 24.1–14
Tuesday **17 January** Antony of Egypt, hermit, abbot, 356 (see p.88) *Charles Gore, bishop, founder of the Community of the Resurrection, 1932* W	Hebrews 6.10–end Psalm 111 Mark 2.23–end	Psalms 132, 147.1–12 or 106* (or 103) Amos 7 1 Corinthians 6.12–end	Psalm 89.1–37 or 107* Genesis 7.11–end Matthew 24.15–28
Wednesday **18 January** **Week of Prayer for Christian Unity: 18–25 January** *Amy Carmichael, founder of the Dohnavur Fellowship, spiritual writer, 1951* W	Hebrews 7.1–3, 15–17 Psalm 110.1–4 Mark 3.1–6	Psalms 81, 147.13–end or 110, 111, 112 Amos 8 1 Corinthians 7.1–24	Psalms 97, 98 or 119.129–152 Genesis 8.1–14 Matthew 24.29–end
Thursday **19 January** *Wulfstan, bishop, 1095 (see p.87)* W	Hebrews 7.25–8.6 Psalm 40.7–10, 17–end Mark 3.7–12	Psalms 76, 148 or 113, 115 Amos 9 1 Corinthians 7.25–end	Psalms 99, 100, 111 or 114, 116, 117 Genesis 8.15–9.7 Matthew 25.1–13
Friday **20 January** *Richard Rolle, spiritual writer, 1349* W	Hebrews 8.6–end Psalm 85.7–end Mark 3.13–19	Psalms 27, 149 or 139 Hosea 1.1–2.1 1 Corinthians 8	Psalms 73 or 130, 131, 137 Genesis 9.8–19 Matthew 25.14–30
Saturday **21 January** *Agnes, child martyr, 304 (see p.85)* Wr	Hebrews 9.2–3, 11–14 Psalm 47.1–8 Mark 3.20–21	Psalms 122, 128, 150 or 120, 121, 122 Hosea 2.2–17 1 Corinthians 9.1–14	Psalms 61, 66 or 118 Genesis 11.1–9 Matthew 25.31–end

		Principal Service	3rd Service	2nd Service
Sunday	**22 January** **3rd Sunday of Epiphany** W	Isaiah 9.1–4 Psalm 27.1, 4–12 [or 27.1–11] 1 Corinthians 1.10–18 Matthew 4.12–23	Psalm 113 Amos 3.1–8 1 John 1.1–4	Psalm 33 [or 33.1–12] Ecclesiastes 3.1–11 1 Peter 1.3–12 HC Luke 4.14–21
		Holy Communion	**Morning Prayer**	**Evening Prayer**
Monday	**23 January** DEL week 3 W	Hebrews 9.15, 24–end Psalm 98.1–7 Mark 3.22–30	Psalms 40, **108** or 123, 124, 125, **126** Hosea 2.18—end of 3 1 Corinthians 9.15–end	Psalms **138**, 144 or **127**, 128, 129 Genesis 11.27—12.9 Matthew 26.1–16
Tuesday	**24 January** Francis de Sales, bishop, teacher of the faith, 1622 (see p.86) W	Hebrews 10.1–10 Psalm 40.1–4, 7–10 Mark 3.31–end	Psalm 34, **36** or **132**, 133 Hosea 4.1–16 1 Corinthians 10.1–13	Psalm **145** or (134,) **135** Genesis 13.2–end Matthew 26.17–35 or: 1st EP of the Conversion of Paul: Psalm 149; Isaiah 49.1–13; Acts 22.3–16
		Principal Service	**3rd Service**	**2nd Service**
Wednesday	**25 January** Conversion of Paul W	Jeremiah 1.4–10 or Acts 9.1–22 Psalm 67 Acts 9.1–22 or Galatians 1.11–16a Matthew 19.27–end	*MP* Psalms 66, 147.13–end Ezekiel 3.22–end Philippians 3.1–14	*EP* Psalm 119.41–56 Ecclesiasticus 39.1–10 or Isaiah 56.1–8 Colossians 1.24—2.7
		Holy Communion	**Morning Prayer**	**Evening Prayer**
Thursday	**26 January** Timothy and Titus, companions of Paul W	Hebrews 10.19–25 Psalm 24.1–6 Mark 4.21–25 *Lesser Festival eucharistic lectionary:* Isaiah 61.1–3a Psalm 100 1 Timothy 2.1–8 or Titus 1.1–5 Luke 10.1–9	Psalms 47, 48 or 143, 146 Hosea 5.8—6.6 1 Corinthians 11.2–16	Psalms 24, 33 or **138**, 140, 141 Genesis 15 Matthew 26.47–56
Friday	**27 January** W	Hebrews 10.32–end Psalm 37.3–6, 40–end Mark 4.26–34	Psalms 61, **65** or 142, 144 Hosea 6.7—7.2 1 Corinthians 11.17–end	Psalms **67**, 77 or **145** Genesis 16 Matthew 26.57–end

If the Presentation of Christ is celebrated on Thursday 2 February:

	Holy Communion	Morning Prayer	Evening Prayer
Saturday **28 January** W Thomas Aquinas, priest, philosopher, teacher of the faith, 1274 (see p.86)	Hebrews 11.1–2, 8–19 Canticle: Luke 1.69–73 Mark 4.35–end	Psalm **68** or **147** Hosea 8 1 Corinthians 12.1–11	Psalms **72**, 76 or **148**, 149, 150 Genesis 17.1–22 Matthew 27.1–10
	Principal Service	**3rd Service**	**2nd Service**
Sunday **29 January** W **4th Sunday of Epiphany**	1 Kings 17.8–16 Psalm 36.5–10 1 Corinthians 1.18–end John 2.1–11	Psalm 71.1–6, 15–17 Haggai 2.1–9 1 Corinthians 3.10–17	Psalm 34 [or 34.1–10] Genesis 28.10–end Philemon 1–16 HC Mark 1.21–28
	Holy Communion	**Morning Prayer**	**Evening Prayer**
Monday **30 January** Wr Charles, king and martyr, 1649 (see p.85) DEL week 4	Hebrews 11.32–end Psalm 31.19–end Mark 5.1–20	Psalms **57**, 96 or 1, 2, 3 Hosea 9 1 Corinthians 12.12–end	Psalms 2, **20** or **4**, 7 Genesis 18.1–15 Matthew 27.11–26
Tuesday **31 January** W John Bosco, priest, founder of the Salesian Teaching Order, 1888	Hebrews 12.1–4 Psalm 22.25b–end Mark 5.21–end	Psalms **93**, 97 or **5**, 6 (8) Hosea 10 1 Corinthians 13	Psalms **19**, 21 or **9**, 10* Genesis 18.16–end Matthew 27.27–44
Wednesday **1 February** W *Brigid, abbess, c.525*	Hebrews 12.4–7, 11–15 Psalm 103.1–2, 13–18 Mark 6.1–6a	Psalms **95**, 98 or **119**.1–32 Hosea 11.1–11 1 Corinthians 14.1–19	1st **EP of the Presentation** Psalm 118 1 Samuel 1.19b–end Hebrews 4.11–end

Epiphany 4 / Presentation

		Principal Service	3rd Service	2nd Service
Thursday	**2 February** *Gold or W* Presentation of Christ in the Temple (Candlemas)	Malachi 3.1–5 Psalm 24.[1–6] 7–end Hebrews 2.14–end Luke 2.22–40	MP Psalms **48**, 146 Exodus 13.1–16 Romans 12.1–5	EP Psalms 122, **132** Haggai 2.1–9 John 2.18–22
		Holy Communion	**Morning Prayer**	**Evening Prayer**
Friday	**3 February** *Gw* Anskar, archbishop, missionary, 865 (see p.88) Ordinary Time begins today The Collect of 5 before Lent is used DEL week 4	Hebrews 13.1–8 Psalm 27.1–6, 9–12 Mark 6.14–29	Psalms 17, **19** Hosea 13.1–14 1 Corinthians 16.1–9	Psalm **22** Genesis 22.1–19 Matthew 28.1–15
Saturday	**4 February** *G* *Gilbert, founder of the Gilbertine Order, 1189*	Hebrews 13.15–17, 20–21 Psalm 23 Mark 6.30–34	Psalms 20, 21, **23** Hosea 14 1 Corinthians 16.10–end	Psalms **24**, 25 Genesis 23 Matthew 28.16–end

			Holy Communion	Morning Prayer	Evening Prayer
Saturday	**28 January** Thomas Aquinas, priest, philosopher, teacher of the faith, 1274 (see p.86)	W	Hebrews 11.1–2, 8–19 *Canticle:* Luke 1.69–73 Mark 4.35–end	Psalm **68** or **147** Hosea 8 1 Corinthians 12.1–11	**1st EP of the Presentation** Psalm 118 1 Samuel 1.19b–end Hebrews 4.11–end
Sunday	**29 January** **Presentation of Christ in the Temple** (Candlemas)	*Gold or* W	**Principal Service** Malachi 3.1–5 Psalm 24.[1–6] 7–end Hebrews 2.14–end Luke 2.22–40	**3rd Service** *MP* Psalms **48**, 146 Exodus 13.1–16 Romans 12.1–5	**2nd Service** *EP* Psalms 122, **132** Haggai 2.1–9 John 2.18–22
Monday	**30 January** Charles, king and martyr, 1649 (see p.85) Ordinary Time begins today The Collect of 5 before Lent is used DEL week 4	Gr	**Holy Communion** Hebrews 11.32–end Psalm 31.19–end Mark 5.1–20	**Morning Prayer** Psalms 1, 2, 3 Hosea 9 1 Corinthians 12.12–end	**Evening Prayer** Psalms **4**, 7 Genesis 18.1–15 Matthew 27.11–26
Tuesday	**31 January** *John Bosco, priest, founder of the Salesian Teaching Order, 1888*	G	Hebrews 12.1–4 Psalm 22.25b–end Mark 5.21–end	Psalms **5**, 6 (8) Hosea 10 1 Corinthians 13	Psalms **9**, 10* Genesis 18.16–end Matthew 27.27–44
Wednesday	**1 February** *Brigid, abbess, c.525*	G	Hebrews 12.4–7, 11–15 Psalm 103.1–2, 13–18 Mark 6.1–6a	Psalm 119.**1–32** Hosea 11.1–11 1 Corinthians 14.1–19	Psalms 11, 12, 13 Genesis 19.1–3, 12–29 Matthew 27.45–56
Thursday	**2 February**	G	Hebrews 12.18–19, 21–24 Psalm 48.1–3, 8–10 Mark 6.7–13	Psalms 14, **15**, 16 Hosea 11.12—end of 12 1 Corinthians 14.20–end	Psalm **18*** Genesis 21.1–21 Matthew 27.57–end
Friday	**3 February** Anskar, archbishop, missionary, 865 (see p.88)	Gw	Hebrews 13.1–8 Psalm 27.1–6, 9–12 Mark 6.14–29	Psalms 17, **19** Hosea 13.1–14 1 Corinthians 16.1–9	Psalm **22** Genesis 22.1–19 Matthew 28.1–15
Saturday	**4 February** *Gilbert, founder of the Gilbertine Order, 1189*	G	Hebrews 13.15–17, 20–21 Psalm 23 Mark 6.30–34	Psalms 20, 21, **23** Hosea 14 1 Corinthians 16.10–end	Psalms **24**, 25 Genesis 23 Matthew 28.16–end

		Principal Service	3rd Service	2nd Service
		Holy Communion	Morning Prayer	Evening Prayer
Sunday	**5 February** G **3rd Sunday before Lent** Proper 1	Isaiah 58.1–9a [9b–12] Psalm 112.1–9 [or Psalm 112] 1 Corinthians 2.1–12 [13–end] Matthew 5.13–20	Psalms 5, 6 Jeremiah 26.1–16 Acts 3.1–10	Psalms [1, 3] 4 Amos 2.4–end Ephesians 4.17–end HC Mark 1.29–39
Monday	**6 February** G *Martyrs of Japan, 1597* Accession of Queen Elizabeth II, 1952 (see p.91) DEL week 5	Genesis 1.1–19 Psalm 104.1, 2, 6–13, 26 Mark 6.53–end	Psalms 27, **30** 2 Chronicles 2.1–16 John 17.1–5	Psalms 26, **28**, 29 Genesis 24.1–28 1 Timothy 6.1–10
Tuesday	**7 February** G	Genesis 1.20–2.4a Psalm 8 Mark 7.1–13	Psalms 32, **36** 2 Chronicles 3 John 17.6–19	Psalm **33** Genesis 24.29–end 1 Timothy 6.11–end
Wednesday	**8 February** G	Genesis 2.4b–9, 15–17 Psalm 104.11–12, 29–32 Mark 7.14–23	Psalm **34** 2 Chronicles 5 John 17.20–end	Psalm 119.**33–56** Genesis 25.7–11, 19–end 2 Timothy 1.1–14
Thursday	**9 February** G	Genesis 2.18–end Psalm 128 Mark 7.24–30	Psalm **37*** 2 Chronicles 6.1–21 John 18.1–11	Psalms 39, **40** Genesis 26.34—27.40 2 Timothy 1.15—2.13
Friday	**10 February** G *Scholastica, abbess, c.543*	Genesis 3.1–8 Psalm 32.1–8 Mark 7.31–end	Psalm 31 2 Chronicles 6.22–end John 18.12–27	Psalm **35** Genesis 27.41—end of 28 2 Timothy 2.14–end
Saturday	**11 February** G	Genesis 3.9–end Psalm 90.1–12 Mark 8.1–10	Psalms 41, **42**, 43 2 Chronicles 7 John 18.28–end	Psalms 45, **46** Genesis 29.1–30 2 Timothy 3

		Principal Service	3rd Service	2nd Service
Sunday	**12 February** **2nd Sunday before Lent** G	Genesis 1.1—2.3 Psalm 136 or Psalm 136.1–9, 23–end Romans 8.18–25 Matthew 6.25–end	Psalms 100, 150 Job 38.1–21 Colossians 1.15–20	Psalm 148 Proverbs 8.1, 22–31 Revelation 4 HC Luke 12.16–31
		Holy Communion	**Morning Prayer**	**Evening Prayer**
Monday	**13 February** DEL week 6 G	Genesis 4.1–15, 25 Psalm 50.1, 8, 16–end Mark 8.11–13	Psalm **44** 2 Chronicles 9.1–12 John 19.1–16	Psalms **47**, 49 Genesis 29.31—30.24 2 Timothy 4.1–8
Tuesday	**14 February** Gw Cyril and Methodius, missionaries, 869 and 885 (see p.88) *Valentine, martyr at Rome, c.269*	Genesis 6.5–8; 7.1–5, 10 Psalm 29 Mark 8.14–21	Psalms **48**, 52 2 Chronicles 10.1—11.4 John 19.17–30	Psalm **50** Genesis 31.1–24 2 Timothy 4.9–end
Wednesday	**15 February** G *Sigfrid, bishop, 1045* *Thomas Bray, priest,* *founder of SPCK and SPG, 1730*	Genesis 8.6–13, 20–end Psalm 116.10–end Mark 8.22–26	Psalm 119.**57–80** 2 Chronicles 12 John 19.31–end	Psalms **59**, 60 (67) Genesis 31.25—32.2 Titus 1
Thursday	**16 February** G	Genesis 9.1–13 Psalm 102.16–23 Mark 8.27–33	Psalms 56, **57** (63*) 2 Chronicles 13.1—14.1 John 20.1–10	Psalms 61, **62**, 64 Genesis 32.3–30 Titus 2
Friday	**17 February** Gr Janani Luwum, archbishop, martyr, 1977 (see p.85)	Genesis 11.1–9 Psalm 33.10–15 Mark 8.34—9.1	Psalms **51**, 54 2 Chronicles 14.2–end John 20.11–18	Psalm **38** Genesis 33.1–17 Titus 3
Saturday	**18 February** G	Hebrews 11.1–7 Psalm 145.1–10 Mark 9.2–13	Psalm **68** 2 Chronicles 15.1–15 John 20.19–end	Psalms 65, **66** Genesis 35 Philemon

Sunday next before Lent

			Principal Service	3rd Service	2nd Service
Sunday	**19 February** **Sunday next before Lent**	G	Exodus 24.12–end Psalm 2 or Psalm 99 2 Peter 1.16–end Matthew 17.1–9	Psalm 72 Exodus 34.29–end 2 Corinthians 4.3–6	Psalm 84 Ecclesiasticus 48.1–10 or 2 Kings 2.1–12 Matthew 17.9–23 (or 1–23)
			Holy Communion	*Morning Prayer*	*Evening Prayer*
Monday	**20 February** DEL week 7	G	Ecclesiasticus 1.1–10 or James 1.1–11 Psalm 93 or 119.65–72 Mark 9.14–29	Psalm 71 Jeremiah 1 John 3.1–21	Psalms 72,75 Genesis 37.1–11 Galatians 1
Tuesday	**21 February**	G	Ecclesiasticus 2.1–11 or James 1.12–18 Psalm 37.3–6, 27–28 or 94.12–18 Mark 9.30–37	Psalm **73** Jeremiah 2.1–13 John 3.22–end	Psalm **74** Genesis 37.12–end Galatians 2.1–10
			Principal Service	*3rd Service*	*2nd Service*
Wednesday	**22 February** **Ash Wednesday**	P(La)	Joel 2.1–2, 12–17 or Isaiah 58.1–12 Psalm 51.1–18 2 Corinthians 5.20b—6.10 Matthew 6.1–6, 16–21 or John 8.1–11	MP Psalm **38** Daniel 9.3–6, 17–19 1 Timothy 6.6–19	EP Psalm **51** or 102 [or 102.1–18] Isaiah 1.10–18 Luke 15.11–end
			Holy Communion	*Morning Prayer*	*Evening Prayer*
Thursday	**23 February** Polycarp, bishop, martyr, c.155 (see p.85)	P(La)r	Deuteronomy 30.15–end Psalm 1 Luke 9.22–25	Psalm **77** or **78.1–39*** Jeremiah 2.14–32 John 4.1–26	Psalm **74** or **78.40–end*** Genesis 39 Galatians 2.11–end
Friday	**24 February**	P(La)	Isaiah 58.1–9a Psalm 51.1–5, 17–18 Matthew 9.14–15	Psalms **3**, 7 or **55** Jeremiah 3.6–22 John 4.27–42	Psalm **31** or **69** Genesis 40 Galatians 3.1–14
Saturday	**25 February**	P(La)	Isaiah 58.9b–end Psalm 86.1–7 Luke 5.27–32	Psalm **71** or **76**,79 Jeremiah 4.1–18 John 4.43–end	Psalm **73** or 81, **84** Genesis 41.1–24 Galatians 3.15–22

		Principal Service	3rd Service	2nd Service
		Holy Communion	Morning Prayer	Evening Prayer
Sunday	**26 February** *P(La)* **1st Sunday of Lent**	Genesis 2.15–17; 3.1–7 Psalm 32 Romans 5.12–19 Matthew 4.1–11	Psalm 119.1–16 Jeremiah 18.1–11 Luke 18.9–14	Psalm 50.1–15 Deuteronomy 6.4–9, 16–end Luke 15.1–10
Monday	**27 February** *P(La)w* George Herbert, priest, poet, 1633 (see p.87)	Leviticus 19.1–2, 11–18 Psalm 19.7–end Matthew 25.31–end	Psalms 10, **11** or **80**, 82 Jeremiah 4.19–end John 5.1–18	Psalms 12, **13**, 14 or **85**, 86 Genesis 41.25–45 Galatians 3.23—4.7
Tuesday	**28 February** *P(La)*	Isaiah 55.10–11 Psalm 34.4–6, 21–22 Matthew 6.7–15	Psalm **44** or 87, **89**.1–18 Jeremiah 5.1–19 John 5.19–29	Psalms 46, **49** or **89**.19–**end** Genesis 41.46–42.5 Galatians 4.8–20
Wednesday	**1 March** *P(La)w* David, bishop, patron of Wales, c.601 (see p.87) Ember Day	Jonah 3 Psalm 51.1–5, 17–18 Luke 11.29–32	Psalms **6**, 17 or 119.**105–128** Jeremiah 5.20–end John 5.30–end	Psalms 9, **28** or **91**, 93 Genesis 42.6–17 Galatians 4.21—5.1
Thursday	**2 March** *P(La)w* Chad, bishop, missionary, 672 (see p.88)	Esther 14.1–5, 12–14 or Isaiah 55.6–9 Psalm 138 Matthew 7.7–12	Psalms **42**, 43 or 90, **92** Jeremiah 6.9–21 John 6.1–15	Psalms 137, 138, **142** or **94** Genesis 42.18–28 Galatians 5.2–15
Friday	**3 March** *P(La)w* Ember Day	Ezekiel 18.21–28 Psalm 130 Matthew 5.20–26	Psalm **22** or **88** (95) Jeremiah 6.22–end John 6.16–27	Psalms 54, **55** or **102** Genesis 42.29–end Galatians 5.16–end
Saturday	**4 March** *P(La)w* Ember Day	Deuteronomy 26.16–end Psalm 119.1–8 Matthew 5.43–end	Psalms 59, **63** or 96, **97**, 100 Jeremiah 7.1–20 John 6.27–40	Psalms **4**, 16 or **104** Genesis 43.1–15 Galatians 6

		Principal Service	3rd Service	2nd Service
Sunday	**5 March** **2nd Sunday of Lent** *P(La)*	Genesis 12.1–4*a* Psalm 121 Romans 4.1–5, 13–17 John 3.1–17	Psalm 74 Jeremiah 22.1–9 Matthew 8.1–13	Psalm 135 [or 135.1–14] Numbers 21.4–9 Luke 14.27–33
		Holy Communion	**Morning Prayer**	**Evening Prayer**
Monday	**6 March** *P(La)*	Daniel 9.4–10 Psalm 79.8–9, 12, 14 Luke 6.36–38	Psalms 26, **32** or **98**, 99, 101 Jeremiah 7.21–end John 6.41–51	Psalms 70, **74** or **105*** (or 103) Genesis 43.16–end Hebrews 1
Tuesday	**7 March** *P(La)r* Perpetua, Felicity and companions, martyrs, 203 (see p.85)	Isaiah 1.10, 16–20 Psalm 50.8, 16–end Matthew 23.1–12	Psalm **50** or **106*** (or 103) Jeremiah 8.1–15 John 6.52–59	Psalm **52**, 53, 54 or **107*** Genesis 44.1–17 Hebrews 2.1–9
Wednesday	**8 March** *P(La)w* Edward King, bishop, 1910 (see p.87) *Felix, bishop, 647* *Geoffrey Studdert Kennedy, priest, poet, 1929*	Jeremiah 18.18–20 Psalm 31.4–5, 14–18 Matthew 20.17–28	Psalm **35** or 110, 111, 112 Jeremiah 8.18—9.11 John 6.60–end	Psalms 3, 51 or **119.129–152** Genesis 44.18–end Hebrews 2.10–end
Thursday	**9 March** *P(La)*	Jeremiah 17.5–10 Psalm 1 Luke 16.19–end	Psalm **34** or 113, **115** Jeremiah 9.12–24 John 7.1–13	Psalm **71** or 114, **116**, 117 Genesis 45.1–15 Hebrews 3.1–6
Friday	**10 March** *P(La)*	Genesis 37.3–4, 12–13, 17–28 Psalm 105.16–22 Matthew 21.33–43, 45–46	Psalms 40, 41 or **139** Jeremiah 10.1–16 John 7.14–24	Psalms **6**, 38 or **130**, 131, 137 Genesis 45.16–end Hebrews 3.7–end
Saturday	**11 March** *P(La)*	Micah 7.14–15, 18–20 Psalm 103.1–4, 9–12 Luke 15.1–3, 11–end	Psalms 3, **25** or 120, **121**, 122 Jeremiah 10.17–24 John 7.25–36	Psalms **23**, 27 or 118 Genesis 46.1–7, 28–end Hebrews 4.1–13

		Principal Service	3rd Service	2nd Service
Sunday	**12 March** *P(La)* **3rd Sunday of Lent**	Exodus 17.1–7 Psalm 95 Romans 5.1–11 John 4.5–42	Psalm 46 Amos 7.10–end 2 Corinthians 1.1–11	Psalm 40 Joshua 1.1–9 Ephesians 6.10–20 *HC* John 2.13–22

The following readings may replace those provided for Holy Communion on any day during the Third Week of Lent:
Exodus 17.1–7; Psalm 95.1–2, 6–end; John 4.5–42

		Holy Communion	Morning Prayer	Evening Prayer
Monday	**13 March** *P(La)*	2 Kings 5.1–15 Psalms 42.1–2; 43.1–4 Luke 4.24–30	Psalms 5, **7** or 123, 124, 125, **126** Jeremiah 11.1–17 John 7.37–52	Psalms 11, **17** or **127**, 128, 129 Genesis 47.1–27 Hebrews 4.14—5.10
Tuesday	**14 March** *P(La)*	Song of the Three 2, 11–20 or Daniel 2.20–23 Psalm 25.3–10 Matthew 18.21–end	Psalms 6, **9** or **132**, 133 Jeremiah 11.18—12.6 John 7.53—8.11	Psalms 61, 62, **64** or (134,) **135** Genesis 47.28—end of 48 Hebrews 5.11—6.12
Wednesday	**15 March** *P(La)*	Deuteronomy 4.1, 5–9 Psalm 147.13–end Matthew 5.17–19	Psalm **38** or **119.153–end** Jeremiah 13.1–11 John 8.12–30	Psalms 36, **39** or **136** Genesis 49.1–32 Hebrews 6.13–end
Thursday	**16 March** *P(La)*	Jeremiah 7.23–28 Psalm 95.1–2, 6–end Luke 11.14–23	Psalms **56**, 57 or **143**, 146 Jeremiah 14 John 8.31–47	Psalms **59**, 60 or **138**, 140, 141 Genesis 49.33—end of 50 Hebrews 7.1–10
Friday	**17 March** *P(La)w* Patrick, bishop, missionary, patron of Ireland, c.460 (see p.88)	Hosea 14 Psalm 81.6–10, 13, 16 Mark 12.28–34	Psalm **22** or 142, **144** Jeremiah 15.10–end John 8.48–end	Psalm **69** or **145** Exodus 1.1–14 Hebrews 7.11–end
Saturday	**18 March** *P(La)* Cyril, bishop, teacher of the faith, 386	Hosea 5.15—6.6 Psalm 51.1–2, 17–end Luke 18.9–14	Psalm **31** or **147** Jeremiah 16.10—17.4 John 9.1–17	Psalms 116, 130 or **148**, 149, 150 Exodus 1.22—2.10 Hebrews 8

Lent 4

		Principal Service	3rd Service	2nd Service
Sunday	**19 March** P(La) **4th Sunday of Lent**	1 Samuel 16.1–13 Psalm 23 Ephesians 5.8–14 John 9	Psalm 19 Isaiah 43.1–7 Ephesians 2.8–14	Psalm 31.1–16 or 31.1–8 Micah 7 or Prayer of Manasseh James 5 HC John 3.14–21

or: 1st EP of Joseph of Nazareth *(transferred to Monday 20 March):*
Psalm 132; Hosea 11.1–9; Luke 2.41–end

For Mothering Sunday:
Exodus 2.1–10 or 1 Samuel 1.20–end; Psalm 34.11–20 or 127.1–4; 2 Corinthians 1.3–7 or Colossians 3.12–17; Luke 2.33–35 or John 19.25b–27
If the Principal Service readings have been displaced by Mothering Sunday provisions, they may be used at the Second Service.
The following readings may replace those provided for Holy Communion on any day during the Fourth Week of Lent (except Joseph of Nazareth or the Feast of the Annunciation):
Micah 7.7–9; Psalm 27.1, 9–10, 16–17; John 9

		Holy Communion		
Monday	**20 March** W Joseph of Nazareth *(transferred from 19 March)*	2 Samuel 7.4–16 Psalm 89.26–36 Romans 4.13–18 Matthew 1.18–end	MP Psalms 25, 147.1–12 Isaiah 11.1–10 Matthew 13.54–end	EP Psalms 1, 112 Genesis 50.22–end Matthew 2.13–end

			Morning Prayer	Evening Prayer
Tuesday	**21 March** P(La)r Thomas Cranmer, archbishop, Reformation martyr, 1556 (see p.85)	Ezekiel 47.1–9, 12 Psalm 46.1–8 John 5.1–3, 5–16	Psalms 54, 79 or 5, 6 (8) Jeremiah 18.1–12 John 10.1–10	Psalms 80, 82 or 9, 10* Exodus 2.23—3.20 Hebrews 9.15–end
Wednesday	**22 March** P(La)	Isaiah 49.8–15 Psalm 145.8–18 John 5.17–30	Psalms 63, 90 or 119.1–32 Jeremiah 18.13–end John 10.11–21	Psalms 52, 91 or 11, 12, 13 Exodus 4.1–23 Hebrews 10.1–18
Thursday	**23 March** P(La)	Exodus 32.7–14 Psalm 106.19–23 John 5.31–end	Psalms 53, 86 or 14, 15, 16 Jeremiah 19.1–13 John 10.22–end	Psalm 94 or 18* Exodus 4.27—6.1 Hebrews 10.19–25
Friday	**24 March** P(La) Walter Hilton, mystic, 1396 Paul Couturier, priest, ecumenist, 1953 Oscar Romero, archbishop, martyr, 1980	Wisdom 2.1, 12–22 or Jeremiah 26.8–11 Psalm 34.15–end John 7.1–2, 10, 25–30	Psalm 102 or 17, 19 Jeremiah 19.14—20.6 John 11.1–16	**1st EP of the Annunciation** Psalm 85 Wisdom 9.1–12 or Genesis 3.8–15 Galatians 4.1–5

		Principal Service	3rd Service	2nd Service
Saturday	**25 March** Gold or W Annunciation of Our Lord to the Blessed Virgin Mary	Isaiah 7.10–14 Psalm 40.5–11 Hebrews 10.4–10 Luke 1.26–38	MP Psalms 111, 113 1 Samuel 2.1–10 Romans 5.12–end	EP Psalms 131, 146 Isaiah 52.1–12 Hebrews 2.5–end

		Principal Service	3rd Service	2nd Service
Sunday	**26 March** **5th Sunday of Lent** *Passiontide begins* P(La)	Ezekiel 37.1–14 Psalm 130 Romans 8.6–11 John 11.1–45	Psalm 86 Jeremiah 31.27–37 John 12.20–33	Psalm 30 Lamentations 3.19–33 Matthew 20.17–end

The following readings may replace those provided for Holy Communion on any day during the Fifth Week of Lent:
2 Kings 4.18–21, 32–37; Psalm 17.1–8, 16; John 11.1–45

		Holy Communion	Morning Prayer	Evening Prayer
Monday	**27 March** P(La)	Susanna 1–9, 15–17, 19–30, 33–62 [or 41b–62] or Joshua 2.1–14 Psalm 23 John 8.1–11	Psalms **73**, 121 or 27, **30** Jeremiah 21.1–10 John 11.28–44	Psalms **26**, 27 or 26, **28**, 29 Exodus 8.1–19 Hebrews 11.17–31
Tuesday	**28 March** P(La)	Numbers 21.4–9 Psalm 102.1–3, 16–23 John 8.21–30	Psalms **35**, 123 or 32, **36** Jeremiah 22.1–5, 13–19 John 11.45–end	Psalms **61**, 64 or **33** Exodus 8.20–end Hebrews 11.32—12.2
Wednesday	**29 March** P(La)	Daniel 3.14–20, 24–25, 28 *Canticle:* Bless the Lord John 8.31–42	Psalms **55**, 124 or **34** Jeremiah 22.20—23.8 John 12.1–11	Psalms 56, **62** or 1 **19**.33–56 Exodus 9.1–12 Hebrews 12.3–13
Thursday	**30 March** P(La)	Genesis 17.3–9 Psalm 105.4–9 John 8.51–end	Psalms **40**, 125 or **37*** Jeremiah 23.9–32 John 12.12–19	Psalms 42, **43** or 39, **40** Exodus 9.13–end Hebrews 12.14–end
Friday	**31 March** P(La) *John Donne, priest, poet, 1631*	Jeremiah 20.10–13 Psalm 18.1–6 John 10.31–end	Psalms **22**, 126 or **31** Jeremiah 24 John 12.20–36a	Psalm **31** or **35** Exodus 10 Hebrews 13.1–16
Saturday	**1 April** P(La) *Frederick Denison Maurice, priest, teacher of the faith, 1872*	Ezekiel 37.21–end *Canticle:* Jeremiah 31.10–13 or Psalm 121 John 11.45–end	Psalms **23**, 127 or 41, **42**, 43 Jeremiah 25.1–14 John 12.36b–end	Psalms 128, 129, **130** or 45, **46** Exodus 11 Hebrews 13.17–end

			Principal Service	3rd Service	2nd Service
Sunday	**2 April** **Palm Sunday**	R	*Liturgy of the Palms:* Matthew 21.1–11 Psalm 118.1–2, 19–end [or 118.19–24] *Liturgy of the Passion:* Isaiah 50.4–9a Psalm 31.9–16 [or 31.9–18] Philippians 2.5–11 Matthew 26.14—end of 27 or Matthew 27.11–54	Psalms 61, 62 Zechariah 9.9–12 Luke 16.19–end	Psalm 80 Isaiah 5.1–7 Matthew 21.33–end
			Holy Communion	**Morning Prayer**	**Evening Prayer**
				From the Monday of Holy Week until the Saturday of Easter Week the seasonal psalmody must be used.	
Monday	**3 April** Monday of Holy Week	R	Isaiah 42.1–9 Psalm 36.5–11 Hebrews 9.11–15 John 12.1–11	Psalm 41 Lamentations 1.1–12a Luke 22.1–23	Psalm 25 Lamentations 2.8–19 Colossians 1.18–23
Tuesday	**4 April** Tuesday of Holy Week	R	Isaiah 49.1–7 Psalm 71.1–14 [or 71.1–8] 1 Corinthians 1.18–31 John 12.20–36	Psalm 27 Lamentations 3.1–18 Luke 22. [24–38] 39–53	Psalm 55.13–24 Lamentations 3.40–51 Galatians 6.11–end
Wednesday	**5 April** Wednesday of Holy Week	R	Isaiah 50.4–9a Psalm 70 Hebrews 12.1–3 John 13.21–32	Psalm 102 [or 102.1–18] Wisdom 1.16—2.1; 2.12–22 or Jeremiah 11.18–20 Luke 22.54–end	Psalm 88 Isaiah 63.1–9 Revelation 14.18—15.4
Thursday	**6 April** Maundy Thursday	W	Exodus 12.1–4 [5–10] 11–14 Psalm 116.1, 10–end [or 116.9–end] 1 Corinthians 11.23–26 John 13.1–17, 31b–35	Psalms 42, 43 Leviticus 16.2–24 Luke 23.1–25	Psalm 39 Exodus 11 Ephesians 2.11–18
Friday	**7 April** Good Friday	*Hangings removed; R for the Liturgy*	Isaiah 52.13—end of 53 Psalm 22 [or 22.1–11 or 22.1–21] Hebrews 10.16–25 or Hebrews 4.14–16; 5.7–9 John 18.1—end of 19	Psalm 69 Genesis 22.1–18 A part of John 18 and 19 may be read, if not used at the Principal Service or Hebrews 10.1–10	Psalms 130, 143 Lamentations 5.15–end John 19.38–end or Colossians 1.18–23

		Principal Service	3rd Service	2nd Service
Saturday	**8 April** **Easter Eve** *These readings are for use at services other than the Easter Vigil.*	*Hangings removed*		
		Job 14.1–14 or Lamentations 3.1–9, 19–24 Psalm 31.1–4, 15–16 [or 31.1–5] 1 Peter 4.1–8 Matthew 27.57–end or John 19.38–end	Psalm 142 Hosea 6.1–6 John 2.18–22	Psalm 116 Job 19.21–27 1 John 5.5–12

		Vigil Readings	Complementary Psalmody	
Saturday **or Sunday**	**8 April evening** **9 April morning** *Easter Vigil* *The New Testament readings should be preceded by a minimum of three Old Testament readings.* *The Exodus reading should always be used.*	*Gold or W*	Genesis 1.1—2.4a Genesis 7.1–5, 11–18; 8.6–18; 9.8–13 Genesis 22.1–18 **Exodus 14.10–end; 15.20–21** Isaiah 55.1–11 Baruch 3.9–15, 32—4.4 or Proverbs 8.1–8, 19–21; 9.4b–6 Ezekiel 36.24–28 Ezekiel 37.1–14 Zephaniah 3.14–end **Romans 6.3–11** **Matthew 28.1–10**	Psalm 136.1–9, 23–end Psalm 46 Psalm 16 **Canticle: Exodus 15.1b–13, 17–18** *Canticle:* Isaiah 12.2–end Psalm 19 Psalms 42, 43 Psalm 143 Psalm 98 **Psalm 114**	

		Principal Service	3rd Service	2nd Service
Sunday	**9 April** **Easter Day**	*Gold or W*	Acts 10.34–43 † or Jeremiah 31.1–6 Psalm 118.1–2, 14–24 [or 118.14–24] Colossians 3.1–4 or Acts 10.34–43† John 20.1–18 or Matthew 28.1–10 † *The reading from Acts must be used as either the first or second reading.*	MP Psalms 114, 117 Exodus 14.10–18, 26—15.2 Revelation 15.2–4	EP Psalm 105 or 66.1–11 Song of Solomon 3.2–5; 8.6,7 John 20.11–18 *if not used at the Principal Service* or Revelation 1.12–18

Easter Week

		Holy Communion	Morning Prayer	Evening Prayer
Monday	**10 April** W Monday of Easter Week	Acts 2.14,22–32 Psalm 16.1–2, 6–end Matthew 28.8–15	Psalms **111**, 117, 146 Song of Solomon 1.9—2.7 Mark 16.1–8	Psalm **135** Exodus 12.1–14 1 Corinthians 15.1–11
Tuesday	**11 April** W Tuesday of Easter Week	Acts 2.36–41 Psalm 33.4–5, 18–end John 20.11–18	Psalms **112**, 147.1–12 Song of Solomon 2.8–end Luke 24.1–12	Psalm **136** Exodus 12.14–36 1 Corinthians 15.12–19
Wednesday	**12 April** W Wednesday of Easter Week	Acts 3.1–10 Psalm 105.1–9 Luke 24.13–35	Psalms **113**, 147.13–end Song of Solomon 3 Matthew 28.16–end	Psalm **105** Exodus 12.37–end 1 Corinthians 15.20–28
Thursday	**13 April** W Thursday of Easter Week	Acts 3.11–end Psalm 8 Luke 24.35–48	Psalms **114**, 148 Song of Solomon 5.2—6.3 Luke 7.11–17	Psalm **106** Exodus 13.1–16 1 Corinthians 15.29–34
Friday	**14 April** W Friday of Easter Week	Acts 4.1–12 Psalm 118.1–4, 22–26 John 21.1–14	Psalms **115**, 149 Song of Solomon 7.10—8.4 Luke 8.41–end	Psalm **107** Exodus 13.17—14.14 1 Corinthians 15.35–50
Saturday	**15 April** W Saturday of Easter Week	Acts 4.13–21 Psalm 118.1–4, 14–21 Mark 16.9–15	Psalms **116**, 150 Song of Solomon 8.5–7 John 11.17–44	Psalm **145** Exodus 14.15–end 1 Corinthians 15.51–end

		Principal Service	3rd Service	2nd Service
Sunday	**16 April** W **2nd Sunday of Easter**	[Exodus 14.10–end; 15.20, 21] Acts 2.14a, 22–32 † Psalm 16 1 Peter 1.3–9 John 20.19–end † *The reading from Acts must be used as either the first or second reading.*	Psalm 81.1–10 Exodus 12.1–17 1 Corinthians 5.6b–8	Psalm 30.1–5 Daniel 6.1–23 or 6.6–23 Mark 15.46—16.8

		Holy Communion	Morning Prayer	Evening Prayer
Monday	**17 April** W	Acts 4.23–31 Psalm 2.1–9 John 3.1–8	Psalms 2, **19** or 1, 2, 3 Deuteronomy 1.3–18 John 20.1–10	Psalm **139** or **4**, 7 Exodus 15.1–21 Colossians 1.1–14
Tuesday	**18 April** W	Acts 4.32–end Psalm 93 John 3.7–15	Psalms **8**, 20, 21 or **5**, 6 (8) Deuteronomy 1.19–40 John 20.11–18	Psalm **104** or **9**, 10* Exodus 15.22—16.10 Colossians 1.15–end
Wednesday	**19 April** Wr Alphege, archbishop, martyr, 1012 (see p.85)	Acts 5.17–26 Psalm 34.1–8 John 3.16–21	Psalms 16, **30** or **119.1–32** Deuteronomy 3.18–end John 20.19–end	Psalm **33** or **11**, 12, 13 Exodus 16.11–end Colossians 2.1–15
Thursday	**20 April** W	Acts 5.27–33 Psalm 34.1, 15–end John 3.31–end	Psalms **28**, 29 or 14, **15**, 16 Deuteronomy 4.1–14 John 21.1–14	Psalm **34** or **18*** Exodus 17 Colossians 2.16—3.11
Friday	**21 April** W Anselm, abbot, archbishop, teacher of the faith, 1109 (see p.86)	Acts 5.34–42 Psalm 27.1–5, 16–17 John 6.1–15	Psalms 57, **61** or 17, **19** Deuteronomy 4.15–31 John 21.15–end	Psalm 118 or **22** Exodus 18.1–12 Colossians 3.12—4.1
Saturday	**22 April** W	Acts 6.1–7 Psalm 33.1–5, 18–19 John 6.16–21	Psalms 63, **84** or 20, 21, **23** Deuteronomy 4.32–40 John 21.20–end	Psalm **66** or **24**, 25 Exodus 18.13–end Colossians 4.2–end

Easter 3

	Principal Service	3rd Service	2nd Service
Sunday W **23 April** **3rd Sunday of Easter**	[Zephaniah 3.14–end] Acts 2.14a, 36–41 † Psalm 116.1–3, 10–end [or 116.1–7] 1 Peter 1.17–23 Luke 24.13–35 † The reading from Acts must be used as either the first or second reading.	Psalm 23 Isaiah 40.1–11 1 Peter 5.1–11	Psalm 48 Haggai 1.13—2.9 1 Corinthians 3.10–17 HC John 2.13–22 or: 1st EP of George, martyr; patron of England: Psalms 111, 116; Jeremiah 15.15–end; Hebrews 11.32—12.2
Monday R **24 April** George, martyr, patron of England, c.304 (transferred from 23 April)	1 Maccabees 2.59–64 or Revelation 12.7–12 Psalm 126 2 Timothy 2.3–13 John 15.18–21	MP Psalms 5, 146 Joshua 1.1–9 Ephesians 6.10–20	EP Psalms 3, 11 Isaiah 43.1–7 John 15.1–8 or: 1st EP of Mark the Evangelist: Psalm 19; Isaiah 52.7–10; Mark 1.1–15
Tuesday R **25 April** Mark the Evangelist	Proverbs 15.28–end or Acts 15.35–end Psalm 119.9–16 Ephesians 4.7–16 Mark 13.5–13	MP Psalms 37.23–end, 148 Isaiah 62.6–10 or Ecclesiasticus 51.13–end Acts 12.25—13.13	EP Psalm 45 Ezekiel 1.4–14 2 Timothy 4.1–11
	Holy Communion	Morning Prayer	Evening Prayer
Wednesday W **26 April**	Acts 8.1b–8 Psalm 66.1–6 John 6.35–40	Psalm 105 or 34 Deuteronomy 6 Ephesians 2.1–10	Psalms 67, 72 or 119.33–56 Exodus 24 Luke 1.39–56
Thursday W **27 April** Christina Rossetti, poet, 1894	Acts 8.26–end Psalm 66.7–8, 14–end John 6.44–51	Psalm 136 or 37* Deuteronomy 7.1–11 Ephesians 2.11–end	Psalm 73 or 39, 40 Exodus 25.1–22 Luke 1.57–end
Friday W **28 April** Peter Chanel, missionary, martyr, 1841	Acts 9.1–20 Psalm 117 John 6.52–59	Psalm 107 or 31 Deuteronomy 7.12–end Ephesians 3.1–13	Psalm 77 or 35 Exodus 28.1–4a, 29–38 Luke 2.1–20
Saturday W **29 April** Catherine of Siena, teacher of the faith, 1380 (see p.86)	Acts 9.31–42 Psalm 116.10–15 John 6.60–69	Psalms 108, 110, 111 or 41, 42, 43 Deuteronomy 8 Ephesians 3.14–end	Psalms 23, 27 or 45, 46 Exodus 29.1–9 Luke 2.21–40

Easter 4

	Principal Service	3rd Service	2nd Service
Sunday **30 April** W **4th Sunday of Easter**	[Genesis 7] Acts 2.42–end † Psalm 23 1 Peter 2.19–end John 10.1–10 † *The reading from Acts must be used as either the first or second reading.*	Psalm 106.6–24 Nehemiah 9.6–15 1 Corinthians 10.1–13	Psalm 29.1–10 Ezra 3.1–13 Ephesians 2.11–end HC Luke 19.37–end *or:* 1st EP of Philip and James, Apostles: Psalm 25; Isaiah 40.27–end; John 12.20–26
Monday **1 May** R Philip and James, Apostles	Isaiah 30.15–21 Psalm 119.1–8 Ephesians 1.3–10 John 14.1–14	MP Psalms 139, 146 Proverbs 4.10–18 James 1.1–12	EP Psalm 149 Job 23.1–12 John 1.43–end
	Holy Communion	**Morning Prayer**	**Evening Prayer**
Tuesday **2 May** W Athanasius, bishop, teacher of the faith, 373 (see p.86)	Acts 11.19–26 Psalm 87 John 10.22–30	Psalm 139 *or* 48 52 Deuteronomy 9.23—10.5 Ephesians 4.17–end	Psalms 115, 116 *or* 50 Exodus 32.15–34 Luke 3.1–14
Wednesday **3 May** W	Acts 12.24—13.5 Psalm 67 John 12.44–end	Psalm 135 *or* 119.57–80 Deuteronomy 10.12–end Ephesians 5.1–14	Psalms 47, 48 *or* 59, 60 (67) Exodus 33 Luke 3.15–22
Thursday **4 May** W English saints and martyrs of the Reformation Era	Acts 13.13–25 Psalm 89.1–2, 20–26 John 13.16–20 *Lesser Festival eucharistic lectionary:* Isaiah 43.1–7 *or* Ecclesiasticus 2.10–17 Psalm 87 2 Corinthians 4.5–12 John 12.20–26	Psalm 118 *or* 56, 57 (63*) Deuteronomy 11.8–end Ephesians 5.15–end	Psalms 81, 85 *or* 61, 62, 64 Exodus 34.1–10, 27–end Luke 4.1–13
Friday **5 May** W	Acts 13.26–33 Psalm 2 John 14.1–6	Psalm 33 *or* 51, 54 Deuteronomy 12.1–14 Ephesians 6.1–9	Psalms 36, 40 *or* 38 Exodus 35.20—36.7 Luke 4.14–30
Saturday **6 May** W	Acts 13.44–end Psalm 98.1–5 John 14.7–14	Psalm 34 *or* 68 Deuteronomy 15.1–18 Ephesians 6.10–end	Psalms 84, 86 *or* 65, 66 Exodus 40.17–end Luke 4.31–37

	Principal Service	3rd Service	2nd Service
	Holy Communion	Morning Prayer	Evening Prayer
Sunday 7 May **5th Sunday of Easter** W	[Genesis 8.1–19] Acts 7.55–end † Psalm 31.1–5, 15–16 [or 31.1–5] 1 Peter 2.2–10 John 14.1–14 † *The reading from Acts must be used as either the first or second reading.*	Psalm 30 Ezekiel 37.1–12 John 5.19–29	Psalm 147.1–12 Zechariah 4.1–10 Revelation 21.1–14 HC Luke 2.25–32 [33–38]
Monday 8 May W Julian of Norwich, spiritual writer, c.1417 (see p.88)	Acts 14.5–18 Psalm 118.1–3, 14–15 John 14.21–26	Psalm 145 or 71 Deuteronomy 16.1–20 1 Peter 1.1–12	Psalm 105 or 72, 75 Numbers 9.15–end; 10.33–end Luke 4.38–end
Tuesday 9 May W	Acts 14.19–end Psalm 145.10–end John 14.27–end	Psalms 19, 147.1–12 or 73 Deuteronomy 17.8–end 1 Peter 1.13–end	Psalms 96, 97 or 74 Numbers 11.1–33 Luke 5.1–11
Wednesday 10 May W	Acts 15.1–6 Psalm 122.1–5 John 15.1–8	Psalms 30, 147.13–end or 77 Deuteronomy 18.9–end 1 Peter 2.1–10	Psalms 98, 99, 100 or 119.81–104 Numbers 12 Luke 5.12–26
Thursday 11 May W	Acts 15.7–21 Psalm 96.1–3, 7–10 John 15.9–11	Psalms 57, 148 or 78.1–39* Deuteronomy 19 1 Peter 2.11–end	Psalm 104 or 78.40–end* Numbers 13.1–3, 17–end Luke 5.27–end
Friday 12 May W Gregory Dix, priest, monk, scholar, 1952	Acts 15.22–31 Psalm 57.8–end John 15.12–17	Psalms 138, 149 or 55 Deuteronomy 21.22—22.8 1 Peter 3.1–12	Psalm 66 or 69 Numbers 14.1–25 Luke 6.1–11
Saturday 13 May W	Acts 16.1–10 Psalm 100 John 15.18–21	Psalms 146, 150 or 76, 79 Deuteronomy 24.5–end 1 Peter 3.13–end	Psalm 118 or 81, 84 Numbers 14.26–end Luke 6.12–26

		Principal Service	3rd Service	2nd Service
Sunday	**14 May** W **6th Sunday of Easter**	[Genesis 8.20—9.17] Acts 17.22–31 † Psalm 66.7–end 1 Peter 3.13–end John 14.15–21 † *The reading from Acts must be used as either the first or second reading.*	Psalm 73.21–28 Job 14.1–2, 7–15; 19.23–27a 1 Thessalonians 4.13–end	Psalms 87, 36.5–10 Zechariah 8.1–13 Revelation 21.22—22.5 HC John 21.1–14
				or: 1st EP of Matthias the Apostle *(transferred to Monday 15 May):* Psalm 147; Isaiah 22.15–22; Philippians 3.13b—4.1
Monday	**15 May** R Matthias the Apostle *(transferred from 14 May)* Rogation Day	Isaiah 22.15–end or Acts 1.15–end Psalm 15 Acts 1.15–end or 1 Corinthians 4.1–7 John 15.9–17	MP Psalms 16, 147.1–12 1 Samuel 2.27–35 Acts 2.37–end	EP Psalm 80 1 Samuel 16.1–13a Matthew 7.15–27
		Holy Communion	**Morning Prayer**	**Evening Prayer**
Tuesday	**16 May** W *Caroline Chisholm, social reformer, 1877* Rogation Day	Acts 16.22-34 Psalm 138 John 16.5-11	Psalms 124, 125, **126**, 127 or 87, **89.1–18** Deuteronomy 28.1–14 1 Peter 4.12–end	Psalms **128**, 129, 130, 131 or **89.19–end** Numbers 16.36–end Luke 6.39–end
Wednesday	**17 May** W Rogation Day	Acts 17.15, 22—18.1 Psalm 148.1–2, 11–end John 16.12–15	Psalms **132**, 133 or 119.**105–128** Deuteronomy 28.58–end 1 Peter 5	**1st EP of Ascension Day** Psalms 15, 24 2 Samuel 23.1–5 Colossians 2.20—3.4

		Principal Service	3rd Service	2nd Service

Thursday 18 May
Ascension Day — Gold or W

Principal Service:
Acts 1.1–11 † or Daniel 7.9–14
Psalm 47 or Psalm 93
Ephesians 1.15–end or Acts 1.1–11 †
Luke 24.44–end
† The reading from Acts must be used as either the first or second reading.

3rd Service:
MP Psalms 110, 150
Isaiah 52.7–end
Hebrews 7.[1–25] 26–end

2nd Service:
EP Psalm 8
Song of the Three 29–37
or 2 Kings 2.1–15
Revelation 5
HC Mark 16.14–end

The nine days after Ascension Day until the eve of Pentecost are observed as days of prayer and preparation for the celebration of the outpouring of the Holy Spirit.
From 19–27 May, in preparation for the Day of Pentecost, an alternative sequence of daily readings for use at the one of the offices is marked with an asterisk*.

	Holy Communion	Morning Prayer	Evening Prayer

Friday 19 May — W
Dunstan, archbishop, monastic reformer, 988 (see p.87)

Holy Communion:
Acts 18.9–18
Psalm 47.1–6
John 16.20–23

Morning Prayer:
Psalms 20, 81 or 88 (95)
Deuteronomy 29.2–15
1 John 1.1—2.6
* Exodus 35.30—36.1; Galatians 5.13–end

Evening Prayer:
Psalm 145 or 102
Numbers 20.1–13
Luke 7.11–17

Saturday 20 May — W
Alcuin, deacon, abbot, 804 (see p.88)

Holy Communion:
Acts 18.22–end
Psalm 47.1–2, 7–end
John 16.23–28

Morning Prayer:
Psalms 21, 47 or 96, 97, 100
Deuteronomy 30
1 John 2.7–17
*Numbers 11.16–17, 24–29; 1 Corinthians 2

Evening Prayer:
Psalms 84, 85 or 104
Numbers 21.4–9
Luke 7.18–35

		Principal Service	3rd Service	2nd Service
Sunday	21 May **7th Sunday of Easter** *Sunday after Ascension Day* W	[Ezekiel 36.24–28] Acts 1.6–14 † Psalm 68.1–10, 32–end [or 68.1–10] 1 Peter 4.12–14; 5.6–11 John 17.1–11 † *The reading from Acts must be used as either the first or second reading.*	Psalm 104.26–35 Isaiah 65.17–end Revelation 21.1–8	Psalm 47 2 Samuel 23.1–5 Ephesians 1.15–end HC Mark 16.14–end

		Holy Communion	Morning Prayer	Evening Prayer
Monday	22 May W	Acts 19.1–8 Psalm 68.1–6 John 16.29–end	Psalms 93, 96, 97 or 98, 99, 101 Deuteronomy 31.1–13 1 John 2.18–end *Numbers 27.15–end; 1 Corinthians 3	Psalm 18 or 105* (or 103) Numbers 22.1–35 Luke 7.36–end
Tuesday	23 May W	Acts 20.17–27 Psalm 68.9–10, 18–19 John 17.1–11	Psalms 98, 99, 100 or 106* (or 103) Deuteronomy 31.14–29 1 John 3.1–10 *1 Samuel 10.1–10; 1 Corinthians 12.1–13	Psalm 68 or 107* Numbers 22.36—23.12 Luke 8.1–15
Wednesday	24 May John and Charles Wesley, evangelists, hymn writers, 1791 and 1788 (see p.87) W	Acts 20.28–end Psalm 68.27–28, 32–end John 17.11–19	Psalms 2, 29 or 110, 111, 112 Deuteronomy 31.30—32.14 1 John 3.11–end *1 Kings 19.1–18; Matthew 3.13–end	Psalms 36, 46 or 119.129–152 Numbers 23.13–end Luke 8.16–25
Thursday	25 May The Venerable Bede, monk, scholar, historian, 735 (see p.88) Aldhelm, bishop, 709 W	Acts 22.30; 23.6–11 Psalm 16.1, 5–end John 17.20–end	Psalms 24, 72 or 113, 115 Deuteronomy 32.15–47 1 John 4.1–6 *Ezekiel 11.14–20; Matthew 9.35—10.20	Psalm 139 or 114, 116, 117 Numbers 24 Luke 8.26–39
Friday	26 May Augustine, archbishop, 605 (see p.87) John Calvin, reformer, 1564 Philip Neri, founder of the Oratorians, spiritual guide, 1595 W	Acts 25.13–21 Psalm 103.1–2, 11–12, 19–20 John 21.15–19	Psalms 28, 30 or 139 Deuteronomy 33 1 John 4.7–end *Ezekiel 36.22–28; Matthew 12.22–32	Psalm 147 or 130, 131, 137 Numbers 27.12–end Luke 8.40–end
Saturday	27 May W	Acts 28.16–20, 30–end Psalm 11.4–end John 21.20–end	Psalms 42, 43 or 120, 121, 122 Deuteronomy 32.48–end, 34 1 John 5 *Micah 3.1–8; Ephesians 6.10–20 (at MP only)	**1st EP of Pentecost** Psalm 48 Deuteronomy 16.9–15 John 15.26—16.15

Pentecost / Ordinary Time

	Principal Service	3rd Service	2nd Service
Sunday 28 May **Pentecost** Whit Sunday R	Acts 2.1–21 † or Numbers 11.24–30 Psalm 104.26–36, 37b [or 104.26–end] 1 Corinthians 12.3b–13 or Acts 2.1–21 † John 20.19–23 or John 7.37–39 † The reading from Acts must be used as either the first or second reading.	MP Psalm 87 Genesis 11.1–9 Acts 10.34–end	EP Psalms 67, 133 Joel 2.21–end Acts 2.14–21 [22–38] HC Luke 24.44–end
	Holy Communion	**Morning Prayer**	**Evening Prayer**
Monday 29 May Ordinary Time resumes today DEL week 8 G	Ecclesiasticus 17.24–29 or James 3.13–end Psalm 32.1–8 or 19.7–end Mark 10.17–27	Psalms 123, 124, 125, **126** 2 Chronicles 17.1–12 Romans 1.1–17	Psalms **127**, 128, 129 Joshua 1 Luke 9.18–27
Tuesday 30 May Josephine Butler, social reformer, 1906 (see p.89) Joan of Arc, visionary, 1431 Apolo Kivebulaya, priest, evangelist, 1933 Gw	Ecclesiasticus 35.1–12 or James 4.1–10 Psalm 50.1–6 or 55.7–9, 24 Mark 10.28–31	Psalms **132**, 133 2 Chronicles 18.1–27 Romans 1.18–end	Psalms (134), **135** Joshua 2 Luke 9.28–36 or: 1st EP of the Visit of the BVM to Elizabeth: Psalm 45; Song of Solomon 2.8–14; Luke 1.26–38
	Principal Service	**3rd Service**	**2nd Service**
Wednesday 31 May Visit of the Blessed Virgin Mary to Elizabeth W	Zephaniah 3.14–18 Psalm 113 Romans 12.9–16 Luke 1.39–49 [50–56]	MP Psalms 85, 150 1 Samuel 2.1–10 Mark 3.31–end	EP Psalms 122, 127, 128 Zechariah 2.10–end John 3.25–30
	Holy Communion	**Morning Prayer**	**Evening Prayer**
Thursday 1 June Justin, martyr, c.165 (see p.85) Gr	Ecclesiasticus 42.15–end or James 5.1–6 Psalm 33.1–9 or 49.12–20 Mark 10.46–end	Psalms **143**, 146 2 Chronicles 20.1–23 Romans 2.17–end	Psalms **138**, 140, 141 Joshua 4.1–5.1 Luke 9.51–end
Friday 2 June G	Ecclesiasticus 44.1, 9–13 or James 5.9–12 Psalm 149.1–5 or 103.1–4, 8–13 Mark 11.11–26	Psalms 142, **144** 2 Chronicles 22.10—end of 23 Romans 3.1–20	Psalm **145** Joshua 5.2–end Luke 10.1–16
Saturday 3 June Martyrs of Uganda, 1885–7, 1977 G	Ecclesiasticus 51.12b–20a or James 5.13–end Psalm 19.7–end or 141.1–4 Mark 11.27–end	Psalm **147** 2 Chronicles 24.1–22 Romans 3.21–end	1st EP of Trinity Sunday Psalms 97, 98 Exodus 34.1–10 Mark 1.1–13

		Principal Service	3rd Service	2nd Service
Sunday 4 June Trinity Sunday	Gold or W	Isaiah 40.12–17, 27–end; Psalm 8; 2 Corinthians 13.11–end; Matthew 28.16–end	*MP* Psalm 86.8–13; Exodus 3.1–6, 13–15; John 17.1–11	*EP* Psalms 93, 150; Isaiah 6.1–8; John 16.5–15
Monday 5 June Boniface (Wynfrith), bishop, martyr, 754 (see p.85) DEL week 9	Gr	**Holy Communion** Tobit 1.1, 2, 2.1–8 or 1 Peter 1.3–9; Psalm 15 or 111; Mark 12.1–12	**Morning Prayer** Psalms 1, 2, 3; 2 Chronicles 26.1–21; Romans 4.1–12	**Evening Prayer** Psalms 4, 7; Joshua 7.1–15; Luke 10.25–37
Tuesday 6 June *Ini Kopuria, founder of the Melanesian Brotherhood, 1945*	G	Tobit 2.9–end or 1 Peter 1.10–16; Psalm 112 or 98.1–5; Mark 12.13–17	Psalms 5, 6 (8); 2 Chronicles 28; Romans 4.13–end	Psalms **9**, 10*; Joshua 7.16–end; Luke 10.38–end

If Corpus Christi is kept as a Festival:

		Principal Service	3rd Service	2nd Service
Wednesday 7 June	G	**Holy Communion** Tobit 3.1–11, 16–end or 1 Peter 1.18–25; Psalm 25.1–8 or 147.13–end; Mark 12.18–27	**Morning Prayer** Psalm **119**.1–32; 2 Chronicles 29.1–19; Romans 5.1–11	**Evening Prayer** Psalms 11, 12, 13; Joshua 8.1–29; Luke 11.1–13 *or:* 1st EP of Corpus Christi: Psalms 110, 111; Exodus 16.2–15; John 6.22–35
Thursday 8 June Day of Thanksgiving for the Institution of Holy Communion (Corpus Christi)	W	**Principal Service** Genesis 14.18–20; Psalm 116.10–end; 1 Corinthians 11.23–26; John 6.51–58	**3rd Service** *MP* Psalm 147; Deuteronomy 8.2–16; 1 Corinthians 10.1–17	**2nd Service** *EP* Psalms 23, 42, 43; Proverbs 9.1–5; Luke 9.11–17

Trinity Sunday

If Corpus Christi is kept as a Lesser Festival, either these readings or those given above for 8 June on page 43 may be used:

		Holy Communion	Morning Prayer	Evening Prayer
Wednesday	**7 June** G	Tobit 3.1–11, 16–end or 1 Peter 1.18–25 Psalm 25.1–8 or 147.13–end Mark 12.18–27	Psalm 119.1–32 2 Chronicles 29.1–19 Romans 5.1–11	Psalms 11, 12, 13 Joshua 8.1–29 Luke 11.1–13
Thursday	**8 June** Gw *Thomas Ken, bishop, nonjuror, hymn writer, 1711 (see p.87)*	Tobit 6.10–11, 7.1–15, 8.4–8 or 1 Peter 2.2–5, 9–12 Psalm 128 or 100 Mark 12.28–34	Psalms 14, 15, 16 2 Chronicles 29.20–end Romans 5.12–end	Psalm 18* Joshua 8.30–end Luke 11.14–28
Friday	**9 June** Gw *Columba, abbot, missionary, 597 (see p.88)* *Ephrem, deacon, hymn writer, teacher of the faith, 373*	Tobit 11.5–15 or 1 Peter 4.7–13 Psalm 146 or 96.10–end Mark 12.35–37	Psalms 17, 19 2 Chronicles 30 Romans 6.1–14	Psalm 22 Joshua 9.3–26 Luke 11.29–36
Saturday	**10 June** G	Tobit 12.1, 5–15, 20a or Jude 17, 20–25 Psalm 103.1, 8–13 or 63.1–6 Mark 12.38–end	Psalms 20, 21, 23 2 Chronicles 32.1–22 Romans 6.15–end	Psalms 24, 25 Joshua 10.1–15 Luke 11.37–end

or, if Barnabas the Apostle is celebrated on Sunday 11 June,
1st EP of Barnabas the Apostle:
Psalms 1, 15; Isaiah 42.5–12;
Acts 14.8–end

If Barnabas the Apostle **is celebrated on Sunday 11 June:**

		Principal Service	3rd Service	2nd Service
Sunday **11 June** Barnabas the Apostle	R	Job 29.11–16 or Acts 11.19–end Psalm 112 Acts 11.19–end or Galatians 2.1–10 John 15.12–17	*MP* Psalms 100, 101, 117 Jeremiah 9.23–24 Acts 4.32–end	*EP* Psalm 147 Ecclesiastes 12.9–end or Tobit 4.5–11 Acts 9.26–31

		Holy Communion	Morning Prayer	Evening Prayer
Monday **12 June** DEL week 10	G	2 Corinthians 1.1–7 Psalm 34.1–8 Matthew 5.1–12	Psalms 27, **30** 2 Chronicles 33.1–13 Romans 7.1–6	Psalms 26, **28**, 29 Joshua 14 Luke 12.1–12

If Barnabas the Apostle **is transferred to Monday 12 June:**

		Principal Service		3rd Service	2nd Service
Sunday **11 June** **1st Sunday after Trinity** Proper 5	G	*Continuous:* Genesis 12.1–9 Psalm 33.1–12	*Related:* Hosea 5.15—6.6 Psalm 50.7–15 Romans 4.13–end Matthew 9.9–13, 18–26	Psalm 38 Deuteronomy 6.10–end Acts 22.22—23.11	Psalms [39] 41 1 Samuel 18.1–16 Luke 8.41–end or: 1st EP of Barnabas the Apostle: Psalms 1, 15; Isaiah 42.5–12; Acts 14.8–end
Monday **12 June** Barnabas the Apostle *(transferred from 11 June)*	R	Job 29.11–16 or Acts 11.19–end Psalm 112 Acts 11.19–end or Galatians 2.1–10 John 15.12–17		*MP* Psalms 100, 101, 117 Jeremiah 9.23–24 Acts 4.32–end	*EP* Psalm 147 Ecclesiastes 12.9–end or Tobit 4.5–11 Acts 9.26–31

		Holy Communion	Morning Prayer	Evening Prayer
Tuesday	**13 June** G DEL week 10	2 Corinthians 1.18–22 Psalm 119.129–136 Matthew 5.13–16	Psalms 32, **36** 2 Chronicles 34.1–18 Romans 7.7–end	Psalm **33** Joshua 21.43—22.8 Luke 12.13–21
Wednesday	**14 June** G *Richard Baxter, puritan divine, 1691*	2 Corinthians 3.4–11 Psalm 78.1–4 Matthew 5.17–19	Psalm **34** 2 Chronicles 34.19–end Romans 8.1–11	Psalm **119.33–56** Joshua 22.9–end Luke 12.22–31
Thursday	**15 June** G *Evelyn Underhill, spiritual writer, 1941*	2 Corinthians 3.15—4.1, 3–6 Psalm 78.36–40 Matthew 5.20–26	Psalm **37*** 2 Chronicles 35.1–19 Romans 8.12–17	Psalms 39, **40** Joshua 23 Luke 12.32–40
Friday	**16 June** Gw Richard, bishop, 1253 (see p.87) *Joseph Butler, bishop, philosopher, 1752*	2 Corinthians 4.7–15 Psalm 99 Matthew 5.27–32	Psalm **31** 2 Chronicles 35.20—36.10 Romans 8.18–30	Psalms **35** Joshua 24.1–28 Luke 12.41–48
Saturday	**17 June** G *Samuel and Henrietta Barnett,* *social reformers, 1913 and 1936*	2 Corinthians 5.14–end Psalm 103.1–12 Matthew 5.33–37	Psalms 41, **42**, **43** 2 Chronicles 36.11–end Romans 8.31–end	Psalms 45, **46** Joshua 24.29–end Luke 12.49–end

		Principal Service	3rd Service	2nd Service
Sunday	G **18 June** **2nd Sunday after Trinity** Proper 6	*Continuous:* Genesis 18.1–15 [21.1–7] Psalm 116.1, 10–17 [or 116.9–17] *Related:* Exodus 19.2–8a Psalm 100 Romans 5.1–8 Matthew 9.35—10.8 [9–23]	Psalm 45 Deuteronomy 10.12—11.1 Acts 23.12–end	Psalms [42] 43 1 Samuel 21.1–15 Luke 11.14–28

		Holy Communion	Morning Prayer	Evening Prayer
Monday	G **19 June** *Sundar Singh, sadhu (holy man), evangelist, teacher of the faith, 1929* DEL week 11	2 Corinthians 6.1–10 Psalm 98 Matthew 5.38–42	Psalm **44** Ezra 1 Romans 9.1–18	Psalms **47**, 49 Judges 2 Luke 13.1–9
Tuesday	G **20 June**	2 Corinthians 8.1–9 Psalm 146 Matthew 5.43–end	Psalms **48**, 52 Ezra 3 Romans 9.19–end	Psalm **50** Judges 4.1–23 Luke 13.10–21
Wednesday	G **21 June**	2 Corinthians 9.6–11 Psalm 112 Matthew 6.1–6, 16–18	Psalm **119.57–80** Ezra 4.1–5 Romans 10.1–10	Psalms **59**, 60 (67) Judges 5 Luke 13.22–end
Thursday	Gr **22 June** Alban, first martyr of Britain, c.250 (see p.85)	2 Corinthians 11.1–11 Psalm 111 Matthew 6.7–15	Psalms **56**, **57** (63*) Ezra 4.7–end Romans 10.11–end	Psalms 61, **62**, 64 Judges 6.1–24 Luke 14.1–11
Friday	Gw **23 June** Etheldreda, abbess, c.678 (see p.88)	2 Corinthians 11.18, 21b–30 Psalm 34.1–6 Matthew 6.19–23	Psalm **51**, 54 Ezra 5 Romans 11.1–12	Psalm **38** Judges 6.25–end Luke 14.12–24 *or:* 1st EP of the Birth of John the Baptist: Psalm 71; Judges 13.2–7, 24–end; Luke 1.5–25

		Principal Service	3rd Service	2nd Service
Saturday	W **24 June** Birth of John the Baptist	Isaiah 40.1–11 Psalm 85.7–end Acts 13.14b–26 or Galatians 3.23–end Luke 1.57–66, 80	*MP* Psalms 50, 149 Ecclesiasticus 48.1–10 or Malachi 3.1–6 Luke 3.1–17	*EP* Psalms 80, 82 Malachi 4 Matthew 11.2–19

Trinity 3

		Principal Service	3rd Service	2nd Service
Sunday	**25 June** G **3rd Sunday after Trinity** Proper 7	*Continuous:* Genesis 21.8–21 Psalm 86.1–10, 16–end [or 86.1–10] *Related:* Jeremiah 20.7–13 Psalm 69.8–11 [12–17] 18–20 [or 69.14–20] Romans 6.1b–11 Matthew 10.24–39	Psalm 49 Deuteronomy 11.1–15 Acts 27.1–12	Psalms 46 [48] 1 Samuel 24.1–17 Luke 14.12–24
		Holy Communion	**Morning Prayer**	**Evening Prayer**
Monday	**26 June** G DEL week 12	Genesis 12.1–9 Psalm 33.12–end Matthew 7.1–5	Psalm 71 Ezra 7 Romans 11.25–end	Psalms 72, 75 Judges 8.22–end Luke 15.1–10
Tuesday	**27 June** G *Cyril, bishop, teacher of the faith, 444*	Genesis 13.2, 5–end Psalm 15 Matthew 7.6, 12–14	Psalm 73 Ezra 8.15–end Romans 12.1–8	Psalm 74 Judges 9.1–21 Luke 15.11–end
Wednesday	**28 June** Gw *Irenaeus, bishop, teacher of the faith, c.200 (see p.86)* Ember Day	Genesis 15.1–12, 17–18 Psalm 105.1–9 Matthew 7.15–20	Psalm 77 Ezra 9 Romans 12.9–end or: 1st EP of Peter and Paul, Apostles [or †Peter the Apostle alone]: Psalms 66, 67; Ezekiel 3.4–11; Galatians 1.13—2.8 [†Acts 9.32–end]	Psalms **119.81–104** Judges 9.22–end Luke 16.1–18
		Principal Service	**3rd Service**	**2nd Service**
Thursday	**29 June** R Peter and Paul, Apostles or Peter the Apostle R	*Peter and Paul:* Zechariah 4.1–6a, 10b–end or Acts 12.1–11 Psalm 125 Acts 12.1–11 or 2 Timothy 4.6–8, 17–18 Matthew 16.13–19 *Peter alone:* Ezekiel 3.22–end or Acts 12.1–11 Psalm 125 Acts 12.1–11 or 1 Peter 2.19–end Matthew 16.13–19	MP Psalms 71, 113 Isaiah 49.1–6 Acts 11.1–18	EP Psalms 124, 138 Ezekiel 34.11–16 John 21.15–22
		Holy Communion	**Morning Prayer**	**Evening Prayer**
Friday	**30 June** G Ember Day	Genesis 17.1, 9–10, 15–22 Psalm 128 Matthew 8.1–4	Psalm 55 Nehemiah 1 Romans 13.8–end	Psalm 69 Judges 11.29–end Luke 17.1–10
Saturday	**1 July** G *Henry, John, and Henry Venn, priests,* *evangelical divines, 1797, 1813, 1873* Ember Day	Genesis 18.1–15 Canticle: Luke 1.46b–55 Matthew 8.5–17	Psalms **76**, 79 Nehemiah 2 Romans 14.1–12	Psalms 81, **84** Judges 2.1–7 Luke 17.11–19

		Principal Service	3rd Service	2nd Service
Sunday	**2 July** **4th Sunday after Trinity** Proper 8	G	*Continuous:* Genesis 22.1–14 Psalm 13 *Related:* Jeremiah 28.5–9 Psalm 89.1–4, 15–18 [or 89.8–18] Romans 6.12–end Matthew 10.40–end	Psalms 52, 53 Deuteronomy 15.1–11 Acts 27.[13–32] 33–end	Psalm 50 [or 50.1–15] 1 Samuel 28.3–19 Luke 17.20–end *or:* 1st EP of Thomas the Apostle: Psalm 27; Isaiah 35; Hebrews 10.35—11.1
Monday	**3 July** Thomas the Apostle	R	Habakkuk 2.1–4 Psalm 31.1–6 Ephesians 2.19–end John 20.24–29	MP Psalms 92, 146 2 Samuel 15.17–21 or Ecclesiasticus 2 John 11.1–16	EP Psalm 139 Job 42.1–6 1 Peter 1.3–12
			Holy Communion	**Morning Prayer**	**Evening Prayer**
Tuesday	**4 July** DEL week 13	G	Genesis 19.15–29 Psalm 26 Matthew 8.23–27	Psalms 87, **89.1–18** Nehemiah 5 Romans 15.1–13	Psalm **89.19–end** Judges 14 Luke 18.1–14
Wednesday	**5 July**	G	Genesis 21.5, 8–20 Psalm 34.1–12 Matthew 8.28–end	Psalm 119.**105–128** Nehemiah 6.1—7.4 Romans 15.14–21	Psalms **91**, 93 Judges 15.1—16.3 Luke 18.15–30
Thursday	**6 July** *Thomas More, scholar, and John Fisher, bishop,* *martyrs, 1535*	G	Genesis 22.1–19 Psalm 116.1–7 Matthew 9.1–8	Psalms 90, **92** Nehemiah 7.73b—end of 8 Romans 15.22–end	Psalm **94** Judges 16.4–end Luke 18.31–end
Friday	**7 July**	G	Genesis 23.1–4, 19; 24.1–8, 62–end Psalm 106.1–5 Matthew 9.9–13	Psalm **88** (95) Nehemiah 9.1–23 Romans 16.1–16	Psalm 102 Judges 17 Luke 19.1–10
Saturday	**8 July**	G	Genesis 27.1–5a, 15–29 Psalm 135.1–6 Matthew 9.14–17	Psalms 96, **97**, 100 Nehemiah 9.24–end Romans 16.17–end	Psalm 104 Judges 18.1–20, 27–end Luke 19.11–27

Trinity 5

		Principal Service		3rd Service	2nd Service
Sunday	9 July G	*Continuous:*	*Related:*	Psalm 55.1–15,18–22	Psalm 56 [57]
	5th Sunday after Trinity	Genesis 24.34-38, 42-49,	Zechariah 9.9–12	Deuteronomy 24.10–end	2 Samuel 2.1–11; 3.1
	Proper 9	58–end	Psalm 145.8–15	Acts 28.1–16	Luke 18.31—19.10
		Psalm 45.10–end or *Canticle:*			
		Song of Solomon 2.8–13			
		Romans 7.15–25a			
		Matthew 11.16–19, 25–end			

		Holy Communion	Morning Prayer	Evening Prayer
Monday	10 July G	Genesis 28.10-end	Psalms **98**, 99, 101	Psalm **105*** (or 103)
	DEL week 14	Psalm 91.1–10	Nehemiah 12.27-47	1 Samuel 1.1–20
		Matthew 9.18–26	2 Corinthians 1.1–14	Luke 19.28–40
Tuesday	11 July Gw	Genesis 32.22-end	Psalm **106*** (or 103)	Psalm **107***
	Benedict, abbot, c.550 (see p.88)	Psalm 17.1–8	Nehemiah 13.1-14	1 Samuel 1.21—2.11
		Matthew 9.32-end	2 Corinthians 1.15—2.4	Luke 19.41-end
Wednesday	12 July G	Genesis 41.55-end; 42.5-7, 17-end	Psalms 110, **111**, 112	Psalm 119.**129–152**
		Psalm 33.1–4, 18-end	Nehemiah 13.15-end	1 Samuel 2.12–26
		Matthew 10.1–7	2 Corinthians 2.5-end	Luke 20.1–8
Thursday	13 July G	Genesis 44.18-21, 23-29; 45.1-5	Psalms 113, **115**	Psalms 114, **116**, 117
		Psalm 105.11–17	Esther 1	1 Samuel 2.27-end
		Matthew 10.7–15	2 Corinthians 3	Luke 20.9–19
Friday	14 July Gw	Genesis 46.1-7, 28-30	Psalm 139	Psalms **130**, 131, 137
	John Keble, priest, poet, 1866 (see p.87)	Psalm 37.3-6, 27-28	Esther 2	1 Samuel 3.1—4.1a
		Matthew 10.16-23	2 Corinthians 4	Luke 20.20–26
Saturday	15 July Gw	Genesis 49.29-end; 50.15-25	Psalms 120, **121**, 122	Psalm 118
	Swithun, bishop, c.862 (see p.87)	Psalm 105.1–7	Esther 3	1 Samuel 4.1b-end
	Bonaventure, friar, bishop, teacher of the faith, 1274	Matthew 10.24-33	2 Corinthians 5	Luke 20.27–40

			Principal Service	3rd Service	2nd Service
Sunday	G	**16 July** **6th Sunday after Trinity** Proper 10	*Continuous:* Genesis 25.19–end Psalm 119.105–112 *Related:* Isaiah 55.10–13 Psalm 65 [or 65.8–end] Romans 8.1–11 Matthew 13.1–9, 18–23	Psalms 64, 65 Deuteronomy 28.1–14 Acts 28.17–end	Psalms 60 [63] 2 Samuel 7.18–end Luke 19.41—20.8
			Holy Communion	**Morning Prayer**	**Evening Prayer**
Monday	G	**17 July** DEL week 15	Exodus 1.8–14, 22 Psalm 124 Matthew 10.34—11.1	Psalms 123, 124, 125, **126** Esther 4 2 Corinthians 6.1—7.1	Psalms **127**, 128, 129 1 Samuel 5 Luke 20.41—21.4
Tuesday	G	**18 July** *Elizabeth Ferard, deaconess, founder of the Community of St Andrew, 1883*	Exodus 2.1–15 Psalm 69.1–2, 31–end Matthew 11.20–24	Psalms **132**, 133 Esther 5 2 Corinthians 7.2–end	Psalms (134,) **135** 1 Samuel 6.1–16 Luke 21.5–19
Wednesday	Gw	**19 July** *Gregory, bishop, and his sister Macrina, deaconess, teachers of the faith, c.394 and c.379 (see p.86)*	Exodus 3.1–6, 9–12 Psalm 103.1–7 Matthew 11.25–27	Psalm 119.**153–end** Esther 6.1–13 2 Corinthians 8.1–15	Psalm **136** 1 Samuel 7 Luke 21.20–28
Thursday	G	**20 July** *Margaret of Antioch, martyr, 4th cent.* *Bartolomé de las Casas, Apostle to the Indies, 1566*	Exodus 3.13–20 Psalm 105.1, 5, 8–9, 24–27 Matthew 11.28–end	Psalms **143**, 146 Esther 6.14—end of 7 2 Corinthians 8.16—9.5	Psalms **138**, 140, 141 1 Samuel 8 Luke 21.29–end
Friday	G	**21 July**	Exodus 11.10—12.14 Psalm 116.10–end Matthew 12.1–8	Psalms 142, **144** Esther 8 2 Corinthians 9.6–end	Psalm **145** 1 Samuel 9.1–14 Luke 22.1–13 *or:* 1st EP of Mary Magdalene: Psalm 139; Isaiah 25.1–9; 2 Corinthians 1.3–7
			Principal Service	**3rd Service**	**2nd Service**
Saturday	W	**22 July** Mary Magdalene	Song of Solomon 3.1–4 Psalm 42.1–10 2 Corinthians 5.14–17 John 20.1–2, 11–18	MP Psalms 30, 32, 150 1 Samuel 16.14–end Luke 8.1–3	EP Psalm 63 Zephaniah 3.14–end Mark 15.40—16.7

Trinity 7

		Principal Service		3rd Service	2nd Service
Sunday	**23 July** G **7th Sunday after Trinity** Proper 11	*Continuous:* Genesis 28.10–19a Psalm 139.1–11, 23–24 [or 139.1–11] Romans 8.12–25 Matthew 13.24–30, 36–43	*Related:* Wisdom 12.13, 16–19 or Isaiah 44.6–8 Psalm 86.11–end	Psalm 71 Deuteronomy 30.1–10 1 Peter 3.8–18	Psalms 67 [70] 1 Kings 2.10–12; 3.16–end Acts 4.1–22 HC Mark 6.30–34, 53–end
		Holy Communion		**Morning Prayer**	**Evening Prayer**
Monday	**24 July** G DEL week 16	Exodus 14.5–18 Psalm 136.1–4, 10–15 or *Canticle:* Exodus 15.1–6 Matthew 12.38–42		Psalms 1, 2, 3 Jeremiah 26 2 Corinthians 11.1–15	Psalms 4, 7 1 Samuel 10.1–16 Luke 22.24–30 or: 1st EP of James the Apostle: Psalm 144; Deuteronomy 30.11–end; Mark 5.21–end
		Principal Service		**3rd Service**	**2nd Service**
Tuesday	**25 July** R James the Apostle	Jeremiah 45.1–5 or Acts 11.27—12.2 Psalm 126 Acts 11.27—12.2 or 2 Corinthians 4.7–15 Matthew 20.20–28		MP Psalms 7, 29, 117 2 Kings 1.9–15 Luke 9.46–56	EP Psalm 94 Jeremiah 26.1–15 Mark 1.14–20

	Holy Communion	Morning Prayer	Evening Prayer
Wednesday 26 July Gw Anne and Joachim, parents of the Blessed Virgin Mary	Exodus 16.1–5, 9–15 Psalm 78.17–31 Matthew 13.1–9 *Lesser Festival eucharistic lectionary:* Zephaniah 3.14–18a Psalm 127 Romans 8.28–30 Matthew 13.16–17	Psalm 1**19.1–32** Jeremiah 29.1–14 2 Corinthians 12	Psalms 11, 12, 13 1 Samuel 11 Luke 22.39–46
Thursday 27 July G *Brooke Foss Westcott, bishop, teacher of the faith, 1901*	Exodus 19.1–2, 9–11, 16–20 *Canticle:* Bless the Lord Matthew 13.10–17	Psalms 14, **15**, 16 Jeremiah 30.1–11 2 Corinthians 13	Psalm **18*** 1 Samuel 12 Luke 22.47–62
Friday 28 July G	Exodus 20.1–17 Psalm 19.7–11 Matthew 13.18–23	Psalms 17, **19** Jeremiah 30.12–22 James 1.1–11	Psalm **22** 1 Samuel 13.5–18 Luke 22.63–end
Saturday 29 July Gw Mary, Martha and Lazarus, companions of Our Lord	Exodus 24.3–8 Psalm 50.1–6, 14–15 Matthew 13.24–30 *Lesser Festival eucharistic lectionary:* Isaiah 25.6–9 Psalm 49.5–10, 16 Hebrews 2.10–15 John 12.1–8	Psalms 20, 21, **23** Jeremiah 31.1–22 James 1.12–end	Psalms **24**, 25 1 Samuel 13.19—14.15 Luke 23.1–12

	Principal Service		3rd Service	2nd Service
	Continuous:	*Related:*		
Sunday 30 July **8th Sunday after Trinity** Proper 12 — G	Genesis 29.15–28 Psalm 105.1–11, 45b [or 105.1–11] or Psalm 128 Romans 8.26–end Matthew 13.31–33, 44–52	1 Kings 3.5–12 Psalm 119.129–136	Psalm 77 Song of Solomon 2 or 1 Maccabees 2.[1–14] 15–22 1 Peter 4.7–14	Psalms 75 [76] 1 Kings 6.11–14, 23–end Acts 12.1–17 HC John 6.1–21

	Holy Communion	Morning Prayer	Evening Prayer
Monday 31 July *Ignatius of Loyola, founder of the Society of Jesus, 1556* DEL week 17 — G	Exodus 32.15–24, 30–34 Psalm 106.19–23 Matthew 13.31–35	Psalms 27, **30** Jeremiah 31.23–25, 27–37 James 2.1–13	Psalms 26, **28**, 29 1 Samuel 14.24–46 Luke 23.13–25
Tuesday 1 August — G	Exodus 33.7–11; 34.5–9, 28 Psalm 103.8–12 Matthew 13.36–43	Psalms 32, **36** Jeremiah 32.1–15 James 2.14–end	Psalm 33 1 Samuel 15.1–23 Luke 23.26–43
Wednesday 2 August — G	Exodus 34.29–end Psalm 99 Matthew 13.44–46	Psalm 34 Jeremiah 33.1–13 James 3	Psalm 1**19.33–56** 1 Samuel 16 Luke 23.44–56a
Thursday 3 August — G	Exodus 40.16–21, 34–end Psalm 84.1–6 Matthew 13.47–53	Psalm 37* Jeremiah 33.14–end James 4.1–12	Psalms 39, **40** 1 Samuel 17.1–30 Luke 23.56b—24.12
Friday 4 August *Jean-Baptiste Vianney, curé d'Ars, spiritual guide, 1859* — G	Leviticus 23.1, 4–11, 15–16, 27, 34–37 Psalm 81.1–8 Matthew 13.54–end	Psalm 31 Jeremiah 35 James 4.13—5.6	Psalm 35 1 Samuel 17.31–54 Luke 24.13–35
Saturday 5 August *Oswald, king, martyr, 642 (see p.85)* — Gr	Leviticus 25.1, 8–17 Psalm 67 Matthew 14.1–12	Psalms 41, **42**, 43 Jeremiah 36.1–18 James 5.7–end	Psalms 45, **46** 1 Samuel 17.55—18.16 Luke 24.36–end *or, if the Transfiguration of Our Lord is celebrated on Sunday 6 August, 1st EP of the Transfiguration of Our Lord:* Psalms 99, 110; Exodus 24.12–end; John 12.27–36a

If The Transfiguration of Our Lord is celebrated on Sunday 6 August:

		Principal Service	3rd Service	2nd Service
Sunday	**6 August** Transfiguration of Our Lord *Gold or W*	Daniel 7.9–10, 13–14 Psalm 97 2 Peter 1.16–19 Luke 9.28–36	MP Psalms 27, 150 Ecclesiasticus 48.1–10 or 1 Kings 19.1–16 1 John 3.1–3	EP Psalm 72 Exodus 34.29–end 2 Corinthians 3
		Holy Communion	**Morning Prayer**	**Evening Prayer**
Monday	**7 August** John Mason Neale, priest, hymn writer, 1866 DEL week 18 *G*	Numbers 11.4–15 Psalm 81.11–end Matthew 14.13–21 or 14.22–end	Psalm 44 Jeremiah 36.19–end Mark 1.1–13	Psalms 47, 49 1 Samuel 19.1–18 Acts 1.1–14

If The Transfiguration of Our Lord is transferred to Monday 7 August:

		Principal Service	3rd Service	2nd Service
Sunday	**6 August** 9th Sunday after Trinity Proper 13 *G*	*Continuous:* Genesis 32.22–31 Psalm 17.1–7, 16 [or 17.1–7] *Related:* Isaiah 55.1–5 Psalm 145.8–9, 15–end [or 145.15–end] Romans 9.1–5 Matthew 14.13–21	Psalm 85 Song of Solomon 5.2–end or 1 Maccabees 3.1–12 2 Peter 1.1–15	Psalm 80 [or 80.1–8] 1 Kings 10.1–13 Acts 13.1–13 HC John 6.24–35 *or:* 1st EP of the Transfiguration of Our Lord: Psalms 99, 110; Exodus 24.12–end; John 12.27–36a
Monday	**7 August** Transfiguration of Our Lord (*transferred from 6 August*) *Gold or W*	Daniel 7.9–10, 13–14 Psalm 97 2 Peter 1.16–19 Luke 9.28–36	MP Psalms 27, 150 Ecclesiasticus 48.1–10 or 1 Kings 19.1–16 1 John 3.1–3	EP Psalm 72 Exodus 34.29–end 2 Corinthians 3

Trinity 9

			Holy Communion	Morning Prayer	Evening Prayer
Tuesday	8 August Dominic, priest, founder of the Order of Preachers, 1221 (see p.88) DEL week 18	Gw	Numbers 12.1–13 Psalm 51.1–8 Matthew 14.22–end or 15.1–2, 10–14	Psalms 48, 52 Jeremiah 37 Mark 1.14–20	Psalm 50 1 Samuel 20.1–17 Acts 1.15–end
Wednesday	9 August Mary Sumner, founder of the Mothers' Union, 1921 (see p.89)	Gw	Numbers 13.1–2, 25—14.1, 26–35 Psalm 106.14–24 Matthew 15.21–28	Psalm 119.57–80 Jeremiah 38.1–13 Mark 1.21–28	Psalms 59, 60 (67) 1 Samuel 20.18–end Acts 2.1–21
Thursday	10 August Laurence, deacon, martyr, 258 (see p.85)	Gr	Numbers 20.1–13 Psalm 95.1–8 Matthew 16.13–23	Psalms 56, 57 (63*) Jeremiah 38.14–end Mark 1.29–end	Psalms 61, 62, 64 1 Samuel 21.1—22.5 Acts 2.22–36
Friday	11 August Clare of Assisi, founder of the Poor Clares, 1253 (see p.88) John Henry Newman, priest, 1890	Gw	Deuteronomy 4.32–40 Psalm 77.11–end Matthew 16.24–end	Psalms 51, 54 Jeremiah 39 Mark 2.1–12	Psalm 38 1 Samuel 22.6–end Acts 2.37–end
Saturday	12 August	G	Deuteronomy 6.4–13 Psalm 18.1–2, 48–end Matthew 17.14–20	Psalm 68 Jeremiah 40 Mark 2.13–22	Psalms 65, 66 1 Samuel 23 Acts 3.1–10

			Principal Service	3rd Service	2nd Service
Sunday	**13 August** **10th Sunday after Trinity** Proper 14	G	*Continuous:* Genesis 37.1–4, 12–28 Psalm 105.1–6, 16–22, 45b [or 105.1–10] *Related:* 1 Kings 19.9–18 Psalm 85.8–13 Romans 10.5–15 Matthew 14.22–33	Psalm 88 Song of Solomon 8.5–7 or 1 Maccabees 14.4–15 2 Peter 3.8–13	Psalm 86 1 Kings 11.41—12.20 Acts 14.8–20 HC John 6.35, 41–51

			Holy Communion	Morning Prayer	Evening Prayer
Monday	**14 August** Maximilian Kolbe, *friar, martyr, 1941* DEL week 19	G	Deuteronomy 10.12–end Psalm 147.13–end Matthew 17.22–end	Psalm 71 Jeremiah 41 Mark 2.23—3.6	Psalms 72, 75 1 Samuel 24 Acts 3.11–end or: 1st EP of the Blessed Virgin Mary: Psalm 72; Proverbs 8.22–23; John 19.23–27

			Principal Service	3rd Service	2nd Service
Tuesday	**15 August** The Blessed Virgin Mary	W	Isaiah 61.10–end or Revelation 11.19—12.6, 10 Psalm 45.10–end Galatians 4.4–7 Luke 1.46–55	MP Psalms 98, 138, 147.1–12 Isaiah 7.10–15 Luke 11.27–28	EP Psalm 132 Song of Solomon 2.1–7 Acts 1.6–14

			Holy Communion	Morning Prayer	Evening Prayer
Wednesday	**16 August**	G	Deuteronomy 34 Psalm 66.14–end Matthew 18.15–20	Psalm 77 Jeremiah 43 Mark 3.19b–end	Psalm 119.81–104 1 Samuel 28.3–end Acts 4.13–31
Thursday	**17 August**	G	Joshua 3.7–11, 13–17 Psalm 114 Matthew 18.21—19.1	Psalm 78.1–39* Jeremiah 44.1–14 Mark 4.1–20	Psalm 78.40–end* 1 Samuel 31 Acts 4.32—5.11
Friday	**18 August**	G	Joshua 24.1–13 Psalm 136.1–3, 16–22 Matthew 19.3–12	Psalm 55 Jeremiah 44.15–end Mark 4.21–34	Psalm 69 2 Samuel 1 Acts 5.12–26
Saturday	**19 August**	G	Joshua 24.14–29 Psalm 16.1, 5–end Matthew 19.13–15	Psalms 76, 79 Jeremiah 45 Mark 4.35–end	Psalms 81, 84 2 Samuel 2.1–11 Acts 5.27–end

Trinity 11

		Principal Service	3rd Service	2nd Service
Sunday	**20 August** G 11th Sunday after Trinity Proper 15	*Continuous:* Genesis 45.1–15 Psalm 133	*Related:* Isaiah 56.1, 6–8 Psalm 67	Psalm 92 Jonah 1 or Ecclesiasticus 3.1–15 2 Peter 3.14–end	Psalm 90 [or 90.1–12] 2 Kings 4.1–37 Acts 16.1–15 HC John 6.51–58
		Romans 11.1–2a, 29–32 Matthew 15.[10–20] 21–28			
		Holy Communion	**Morning Prayer**	**Evening Prayer**
Monday	**21 August** G DEL week 20	Judges 2.11–19 Psalm 106.34–42 Matthew 19.16–22		Psalms 80, 82 Micah 1.1–9 Mark 5.1–20	Psalms 85, 86 2 Samuel 3.12–end Acts 6
Tuesday	**22 August** G	Judges 6.11–24 Psalm 85.8–end Matthew 19.23–end		Psalms 87, **89.1–18** Micah 2 Mark 5.21–34	Psalm **89.19–end** 2 Samuel 5.1–12 Acts 7.1–16
Wednesday	**23 August** G	Judges 9.6–15 Psalm 21.1–6 Matthew 20.1–16		Psalm 119.**105–128** Micah 3 Mark 5.35–end	Psalms **91**, 93 2 Samuel 6.1–19 Acts 7.17–43
					or: 1st EP of Bartholomew the Apostle: Psalm 97; Isaiah 61.1–9; 2 Corinthians 6.1–10
		Principal Service	**3rd Service**	**2nd Service**
Thursday	**24 August** R Bartholomew the Apostle	Isaiah 43.8–13 or Acts 5.12–16 Psalm 145.1–7 Acts 5.12–16 or 1 Corinthians 4.9–15 Luke 22.24–30		MP Psalms 86, 117 Genesis 28.10–17 John 1.43–end	EP Psalms 91, 116 Ecclesiasticus 39.1–10 or Deuteronomy 18.15–19 Matthew 10.1–22
		Holy Communion	**Morning Prayer**	**Evening Prayer**
Friday	**25 August** G	Ruth 1.1, 3–6, 14–16, 22 Psalm 146 Matthew 22.34–40		Psalms 88 (95) Micah 5.2–end Mark 6.14–29	Psalm **102** 2 Samuel 7.18–end Acts 7.54—8.3
Saturday	**26 August** G	Ruth 2.1–3, 8–11, 4.13–17 Psalm 128 Matthew 23.1–12		Psalms 96, **97**, 100 Micah 6 Mark 6.30–44	Psalm **104** 2 Samuel 9 Acts 8.4–25

		Principal Service	3rd Service	2nd Service
Sunday	**27 August** G **12th Sunday after Trinity** Proper 16	*Continuous:* Exodus 1.8—2.10 Psalm 124 *Related:* Isaiah 51.1–6 Psalm 138 Romans 12.1–8 Matthew 16.13–20	Psalm 104.1–25 Jonah 2 or Ecclesiasticus 3.17–29 Revelation 1	Psalm 95 2 Kings 6.8–23 Acts 17.15–end *HC* John 6.56–69
		Holy Communion	**Morning Prayer**	**Evening Prayer**
Monday	**28 August** Gw Augustine, bishop, teacher of the faith, 430 (see p.86) DEL week 21	1 Thessalonians 1.1–5, 8–end Psalm 149.1–5 Matthew 23.13–22	Psalms 98, 99, 101 Micah 7.1–7 Mark 6.45–end	Psalm **105*** (or 103) 2 Samuel 11 Acts 8.26–end
Tuesday	**29 August** Gr Beheading of John the Baptist	1 Thessalonians 2.1–8 Psalm 139.1–9 Matthew 23.23–26 *Lesser Festival eucharistic lectionary:* Jeremiah 1.4–10 Psalm 1 Hebrews 11.32—12.2 Matthew 14.1–12	Psalm **106*** (or 103) Micah 7.8–end Mark 7.1–13	Psalm **107*** 2 Samuel 12.1–25 Acts 9.1–19a
Wednesday	**30 August** Gw John Bunyan, spiritual writer, 1688 (see p.86)	1 Thessalonians 2.9–13 Psalm 126 Matthew 23.27–32	Psalms 110, **111**, 112 Habakkuk 1.1–11 Mark 7.14–23	Psalm **119.129–152** 2 Samuel 15.1–12 Acts 9.19b–31
Thursday	**31 August** Gw Aidan, bishop, missionary, 651 (see p.88)	1 Thessalonians 3.7–end Psalm 90.13–end Matthew 24.42–end	Psalms 113, **115** Habakkuk 1.12—2.5 Mark 7.24–30	Psalms 114, **116**, 117 2 Samuel 15.13–end Acts 9.32–end
Friday	**1 September** G *Giles, hermit, c.710*	1 Thessalonians 4.1–8 Psalm 97 Matthew 25.1–13	Psalm **139** Habakkuk 2.6–end Mark 7.31–end	Psalms 130, 131, 137 2 Samuel 16.1–14 Acts 10.1–16
Saturday	**2 September** G *Martyrs of Papua New Guinea, 1901, 1942*	1 Thessalonians 4.9–12 Psalm 98.1–2, 8–end Matthew 25.14–30	Psalms 120, **121**, 122 Habakkuk 3.2–19a Mark 8.1–10	Psalm 118 2 Samuel 17.1–23 Acts 10.17–33

		Principal Service		3rd Service	2nd Service
Sunday	**3 September** **13th Sunday after Trinity** Proper 17	G	*Continuous:* Exodus 3.1–15 Psalm 105.1–6, 23–26, 45b [or Psalm 115] *Related:* Jeremiah 15.15–21 Psalm 26.1–8 Romans 12.9–end Matthew 16.21–end	Psalm 107.1–32 Jonah 3.1–9 or Ecclesiasticus 11.7–28 [or 19–28] Revelation 3.14–end	Psalm 105.1–15 2 Kings 6.24–25; 7.3–end Acts 18.1–16 HC Mark 7.1–8, 14–15, 21–23
		Holy Communion		**Morning Prayer**	**Evening Prayer**
Monday	**4 September** *Birinus, bishop, 650* DEL week 22	G	1 Thessalonians 4.13–end Psalm 96 Luke 4.16–30		Psalms 123, 124, 125, **126** Haggai 1.1–11 Mark 8.11–21	Psalms **127**, 128, 129 2 Samuel 18.1–18 Acts 10.34–end
Tuesday	**5 September**	G	1 Thessalonians 5.1–6, 9–11 Psalm 27.1–8 Luke 4.31–37		Psalms **132**, 133 Haggai 1.12—2.9 Mark 8.22–26	Psalms (134), **135** 2 Samuel 18.19—19.8*a* Acts 11.1–18
Wednesday	**6 September** *Allen Gardiner, missionary, founder of the* *South American Mission Society, 1851*	G	Colossians 1.1–8 Psalm 34.11–18 Luke 4.38–end		Psalm 119.**153–end** Haggai 2.10–end Mark 8.27—9.1	Psalm **136** 2 Samuel 19.8*b*–23 Acts 11.19–end
Thursday	**7 September**	G	Colossians 1.9–14 Psalm 98.1–5 Luke 5.1–11		Psalms **143**, 146 Zechariah 1.1–17 Mark 9.2–13	Psalms **138**, 140, 141 2 Samuel 19.24–end Acts 12.1–17
Friday	**8 September** **Birth of the Blessed Virgin Mary** (see p.85)	Gw	Colossians 1.15–20 Psalm 89.19*b*–28 Luke 5.33–end		Psalms 142, **144** Zechariah 1.18—end of 2 Mark 9.14–29	Psalm **145** 2 Samuel 23.1–7 Acts 12.18–end
Saturday	**9 September** *Charles Fuge Lowder, priest, 1880*	G	Colossians 1.21–23 Psalm 117 Luke 6.1–5		Psalm **147** Zechariah 3 Mark 9.30–37	Psalms **148**, 149, 150 2 Samuel 24 Acts 13.1–12

	Principal Service	3rd Service	2nd Service
Sunday **10 September** 14th Sunday after Trinity Proper 18 — G	*Continuous:* Exodus 12.1–14 Psalm 149 *Related:* Ezekiel 33.7–11 Psalm 119.33–40 Romans 13.8–end Matthew 18.15–20	Psalm 119.17–32 Jonah 3.10—4.11 or Ecclesiasticus 27.30—28.9 Revelation 8.1–5	Psalms 108 [115] Ezekiel 12.21—13.16 Acts 19.1–20 HC Mark 7.24–end

	Holy Communion	Morning Prayer	Evening Prayer
Monday **11 September** DEL week 23 — G	Colossians 1.24—2.3 Psalm 62.1–7 Luke 6.6–11	Psalms 1, 2, 3 Zechariah 4 Mark 9.38–end	Psalms 4, 7 1 Kings 1.5–31 Acts 13.13–43
Tuesday **12 September** — G	Colossians 2.6–15 Psalm 8 Luke 6.12–19	Psalms 5, 6 (8) Zechariah 6.9–end Mark 10.1–16	Psalms 9, 10* 1 Kings 1.32—2.4; 2.10–12 Acts 13.44—14.7
Wednesday **13 September** John Chrysostom, bishop, teacher of the faith, 407 (see p.85) — Gw	Colossians 3.1–11 Psalm 15 Luke 6.20–26	Psalm 119.1–11 Zechariah 7 Mark 10.17–31	Psalms 11, 12, 13 1 Kings 3 Acts 14.8–end *or:* 1st EP of Holy Cross Day: Psalm 66; Isaiah 52.13—end of 53; Ephesians 2.11–end

	Principal Service	3rd Service	2nd Service
Thursday **14 September** Holy Cross Day — R	Numbers 21.4–9 Psalm 22.23–28 Philippians 2.6–11 John 3.13–17	MP Psalms 2, 8, 146 Genesis 3.1–15 John 12.27–36a	EP Psalms 110, 150 Isaiah 63.1–16 1 Corinthians 1.18–25

	Holy Communion	Morning Prayer	Evening Prayer
Friday **15 September** Cyprian, bishop, martyr, 258 (see p.85) — Gr	1 Timothy 1.1–2, 12–14 Psalm 16 Luke 6.39–42	Psalms 17, 19 Zechariah 8.9–end Mark 10.35–45	Psalm 22 1 Kings 6.1, 11–28 Acts 15.22–35
Saturday **16 September** Ninian, bishop, apostle of the Picts, c.432 (see p.88) *Edward Bouverie Pusey, priest, 1882* — Gw	1 Timothy 1.15–17 Psalm 113 Luke 6.43–end	Psalms 20, 21, 23 Zechariah 9.1–12 Mark 10.46–end	Psalms 24, 25 1 Kings 8.1–30 Acts 15.36—16.5

Trinity 15

	Principal Service	3rd Service	2nd Service
Sunday **17 September** G **15th Sunday after Trinity** Proper 19	*Continuous:* Exodus 14.19–end Psalm 114 or *Canticle:* Exodus 15.1b–11, 20–21 Romans 14.1–12 Matthew 18.21–35 *Related:* Genesis 50.15–21 Psalm 103.1–13 [or 103.8–13] Romans 14.1–12 Matthew 18.21–35	Psalm 119.65–88 Isaiah 44.24–45.8 Revelation 12.1–12	Psalm 119.41–48 [49–64] Ezekiel 20.1–8, 33–44 Acts 20.17–end HC Mark 8.27–end

	Holy Communion	Morning Prayer	Evening Prayer
Monday **18 September** G DEL week 24	1 Timothy 2.1–8 Psalm 28 Luke 7.1–10	Psalms 27, **30** Zechariah 10 Mark 11.1–11	Psalms 26, **28**, 29 1 Kings 8.31–62 Acts 16.6–24
Tuesday **19 September** G *Theodore, archbishop, 690*	1 Timothy 3.1–13 Psalm 101 Luke 7.11–17	Psalms 32, **36** Zechariah 11.4–end Mark 11.12–26	Psalm 33 1 Kings 8.63—9.9 Acts 16.25–end
Wednesday **20 September** Gr John Coleridge Patteson, bishop, and companions, martyrs, 1871 (see p.85)	1 Timothy 3.14–end Psalm 111.1–5 Luke 7.31–35	Psalm **34** Zechariah 12.1–10 Mark 11.27–end	Psalm **119.33–56** 1 Kings 10.1–25 Acts 17.1–15 *or:* 1st EP of Matthew, Apostle and Evangelist: Psalm 34; Isaiah 33.13–17; Matthew 6.19–end

	Principal Service	3rd Service	2nd Service
Thursday **21 September** R Matthew, Apostle and Evangelist	Proverbs 3.13–18 Psalm 119.65–72 2 Corinthians 4.1–6 Matthew 9.9–13	MP Psalms 49, 117 1 Kings 19.15–end 2 Timothy 3.14–end	EP Psalm 119.33–40, 89–96 Ecclesiastes 5.4–12 Matthew 19.16–end

	Holy Communion	Morning Prayer	Evening Prayer
Friday **22 September** G	1 Timothy 6.2b–12 Psalm 49.1–9 Luke 8.1–3	Psalm **31** Zechariah 14.1–11 Mark 12.13–17	Psalm **35** 1 Kings 11.26–end Acts 18.1–21
Saturday **23 September** G	1 Timothy 6.13–16 Psalm 100 Luke 8.4–15	Psalms 41, **42**, 43 Zechariah 14.12–end Mark 12.18–27	Psalms 45, **46** 1 Kings 12.1–24 Acts 18.22—19.7

	Principal Service	3rd Service	2nd Service
Sunday 24 September G **16th Sunday after Trinity** Proper 20	*Continuous:* Exodus 16.2–15 Psalm 105.1–6, 37–end [or 105.37–end] *Related:* Jonah 3.10—end of 4 Psalm 145.1–8 Philippians 1.21–end Matthew 20.1–16	Psalm 119.153–end Isaiah 45.9–22 Revelation 14.1–5	Psalm 119.113–136 [or 119.121–[128]] Ezekiel 33.23, 30—34.10 Acts 26.1, 9–25 HC Mark 9.30–37

	Holy Communion	Morning Prayer	Evening Prayer
Monday 25 September Gw *Lancelot Andrewes, bishop,* *spiritual writer, 1626 (see p.87)* *Sergei of Radonezh, monastic reformer,* *teacher of the faith, 1392* DEL week 25	Ezra 1.1–6 Psalm 126 Luke 8.16–18	Psalm **44** Ecclesiasticus 1.1–10 or Ezekiel 1.1–14 Mark 12.28–34	Psalm **47**, 49 1 Kings 12.25—13.10 Acts 19.8–20
Tuesday 26 September G *Wilson Carlile,* *founder of the Church Army, 1942*	Ezra 6.7–8, 12, 14–20 Psalm 124 Luke 8.19–21	Psalms **48**, 52 Ecclesiasticus 1.11–end or Ezekiel 1.15—2.2 Mark 12.35–end	Psalm **50** 1 Kings 13.11–end Acts 19.21–end
Wednesday 27 September Gw *Vincent de Paul, founder of the Lazarists,* *1660 (see p.88)* Ember Day	Ezra 9.5–9 *Canticle:* Song of Tobit or Psalm 103.1–6 Luke 9.1–6	Psalm 119.**57–80** Ecclesiasticus 2 or Ezekiel 2.3—3.11 Mark 13.1–13	Psalms **59**, 60 (67) 1 Kings 17 Acts 20.1–16
Thursday 28 September G	Haggai 1.1–8 Psalm 149.1–5 Luke 9.7–9	Psalms 56, **57** (63*) Ecclesiasticus 3.17–29 or Ezekiel 3.12–end Mark 13.14–23	Psalms 61, **62**, 64 1 Kings 18.1–20 Acts 20.17–end or: 1st EP of Michael and All Angels: Psalm 91; 2 Kings 6.8–17; Matthew 18.1–6, 10

	Principal Service	3rd Service	2nd Service
Friday 29 September W Michael and All Angels Ember Day	Genesis 28.10–17 or Revelation 12.7–12 Psalm 103.19–end Revelation 12.7–12 or Hebrews 1.5–end John 1.47–end	*MP* Psalms 34, 150 Tobit 12.6–end or Daniel 12.1–4 Acts 12.1–11	*EP* Psalms 138, 148 Daniel 10.4–end Revelation 5

	Holy Communion	Morning Prayer	Evening Prayer
Saturday 30 September Gw *Jerome, translator, teacher of the faith, 420* Ember Day	Zechariah 2.1–5, 10–11 Psalm 125 or *Canticle:* Jeremiah 31.10–13 Luke 9.43b–**45**	Psalm **68** Ecclesiasticus 4.29—6.1 or Ezekiel 9 Mark 13.32–end	Psalms 65, **66** 1 Kings 19 Acts 21.17–36

		Principal Service		3rd Service	2nd Service
Sunday	**1 October** **17th Sunday after Trinity** Proper 21	G	*Continuous:* Exodus 17.1–7 Psalm 78.1–4, 12–16 [or 78.1–7]	*Related:* Ezekiel 18.1–4, 25–end Psalm 25.1–8 Philippians 2.1–13 Matthew 21.23–32	Psalms 125, 126, 127 Isaiah 48.12–21 Luke 11.37–54	Psalms [120, 123] 124 Ezekiel 37.15–end 1 John 2.22–end HC Mark 9.38–end

			Holy Communion	Morning Prayer	Evening Prayer
Monday	**2 October** DEL week 26	G		Zechariah 8.1–8 Psalm 102.12–22 Luke 9.46–50	Psalm 71 Ecclesiasticus 6.14–end or Ezekiel 10.1–19 Mark 11.1–11	Psalms 72, 75 1 Kings 21 Acts 21.37—22.21
Tuesday	**3 October** George Bell, bishop, ecumenist, peacemaker, 1958	G		Zechariah 8.20–end Psalm 87 Luke 9.51–56	Psalm 73 Ecclesiasticus 7.27–end or Ezekiel 11.14–end Mark 14.12–25	Psalm 74 1 Kings 22.1–28 Acts 22.22—23.11
Wednesday	**4 October** Francis of Assisi, friar, deacon, 1226 (see p.88)	Gw		Nehemiah 2.1–8 Psalm 137.1–6 Luke 9.57–end	Psalm 77 Ecclesiasticus 10.6–8, 12–24 or Ezekiel 12.1–16 Mark 14.26–42	Psalm 119.81–104 1 Kings 22.29–45 Acts 23.12–end
Thursday	**5 October**	G		Nehemiah 8.1–12 Psalm 19.7–11 Luke 10.1–12	Psalm 78.1–39* Ecclesiasticus 11.7–28 or Ezekiel 12.17–end Mark 14.43–52	Psalm 78.40–end* 2 Kings 1.2–17 Acts 24.1–23
Friday	**6 October** William Tyndale, translator, martyr, 1536 (see p.85)	Gr		Baruch 1.15–end or Deuteronomy 31.7–13 Psalm 79.1–9 Luke 10.13–16	Psalm 55 Ecclesiasticus 14.20—15.10 or Ezekiel 13.1–16 Mark 14.53–65	Psalm 69 2 Kings 2.1–18 Acts 24.24—25.12
Saturday	**7 October**	G		Baruch 4.5–12, 27–29 or Joshua 22.1–6 Psalm 69.33–37 Luke 10.17–24	Psalms 76, 79 Ecclesiasticus 15.11–end or Ezekiel 14.1–11 Mark 14.66–end	Psalms 81, 84 2 Kings 4.1–37 Acts 25.13–end

		Principal Service	3rd Service	2nd Service
Sunday	**8 October** G **18th Sunday after Trinity** Proper 22	*Continuous:* Exodus 20.1–4, 7–9, 12–20 Psalm 19 [or 19.7–end] *Related:* Isaiah 5.1–7 Psalm 80.9–17 Philippians 3.4b–14 Matthew 21.33–end	Psalms 128, 129, 134 Isaiah 49.13–23 Luke 12.1–12	Psalm 136 [or 136.1–9] Proverbs 2.1–11 1 John 2.1–17 *HC* Mark 10.2–16
Monday	**9 October** G *Denys, bishop, and companions, martyrs, c.250* *Robert Grosseteste, bishop, philosopher, scientist, 1253* DEL week 27	**Holy Communion** Jonah 1.1—2.2, 10 Canticle: Jonah 2.2–4, 7 or Psalm 69.1–6 Luke 10.25–37	**Morning Prayer** Psalms 80, 82 Ecclesiasticus 16.17–end or Ezekiel 14.12–end Mark 15.1–15	**Evening Prayer** Psalms 85, 86 2 Kings 5 Acts 26.1–23
Tuesday	**10 October** Gw *Paulinus, bishop, missionary, 644 (see p.88)* *Thomas Traherne, poet, spiritual writer, 1674*	Jonah 3 Psalm 130 Luke 10.38–end	Psalms 87, **89.1–18** Ecclesiasticus 17.1–24 or Ezekiel 18.1–20 Mark 15.16–32	Psalm **89.19–end** 2 Kings 6.1–23 Acts 26.24–end
Wednesday	**11 October** G *Ethelburga, abbess, 675* *James the Deacon, companion of Paulinus, 7th cent.*	Jonah 4 Psalm 86.1–9 Luke 11.1–4	Psalm 119.**105–128** Ecclesiasticus 18.1–14 or Ezekiel 18.21–32 Mark 15.33–41	Psalms 91, 93 2 Kings 9.1–16 Acts 27.1–26
Thursday	**12 October** Gw *Wilfrid, bishop, missionary, 709 (see p.88)* *Elizabeth Fry, prison reformer, 1845* *Edith Cavell, nurse, 1915*	Malachi 3.13—4.2a Psalm 1 Luke 11.5–13	Psalms 90, **92** Ecclesiasticus 19.4–17 or Ezekiel 20.1–20 Mark 15.42–end	Psalm **94** 2 Kings 9.17–end Acts 27.27–end
Friday	**13 October** Gw *Edward the Confessor, king, 1066 (see p.89)*	Joel 1.13–15; 2.1–2 Psalm 9.1–7 Luke 11.15–26	Psalms **88** (95) Ecclesiasticus 19.20–end or Ezekiel 20.21–38 Mark 16.1–8	Psalm **102** 2 Kings 12.1–19 Acts 28.1–16
Saturday	**14 October** G	Joel 3.12–end Psalm 97.1, 8–end Luke 11.27–28	Psalms 96, **97**, 100 Ecclesiasticus 21.1–17 or Ezekiel 24.15–end Mark 16.9–end	Psalm **104** 2 Kings 17.1–23 Acts 28.17–end

Trinity 19

			Principal Service	3rd Service	2nd Service
Sunday	**15 October** **19th Sunday after Trinity** Proper 23	G	*Continuous:* Exodus 32.1–14 Psalm 106.1–6, 19–23 [or 106.1–6] *Related:* Isaiah 25.1–9 Psalm 23 Philippians 4.1–9 Matthew 22.1–14	Psalms 138, 141 Isaiah 50.4–10 Luke 13.22–30	Psalm 139.1–18 [or 139.1–11] Proverbs 3.1–18 1 John 3.1–15 HC Mark 10.17–31

			Holy Communion	Morning Prayer	Evening Prayer
Monday	**16 October** *Nicholas Ridley and Hugh Latimer, bishops, martyrs, 1555* DEL week 28	G	Romans 1.1–7 Psalm 98 Luke 11.29–32	Psalms 98, 99, 101 Ecclesiasticus 22.6–22 or Ezekiel 28.1–19 John 13.1–11	Psalm 105* (or 103) 2 Kings 17.24–end Philippians 1.1–11
Tuesday	**17 October** Ignatius, bishop, martyr, c.107 (see p.85)	Gr	Romans 1.16–25 Psalm 19.1–4 Luke 11.37–41	Psalm 106* (or 103) Ecclesiasticus 22.27—23.15 or Ezekiel 33.1–20 John 13.12–20	Psalm 107* 2 Kings 18.1–12 Philippians 1.12–end or: 1st EP of Luke the Evangelist: Psalm 33; Hosea 6.1–3; 2 Timothy 3.10–end

			Principal Service	3rd Service	2nd Service
Wednesday	**18 October** Luke the Evangelist	R	Isaiah 35.3–6 or Acts 16.6–12a Psalm 147.1–7 2 Timothy 4.5–17 Luke 10.1–9	MP Psalms 145, 146 Isaiah 55 Luke 1.1–4	EP Psalm 103 Ecclesiasticus 38.1–14 or Isaiah 61.1–6 Colossians 4.7–end

			Holy Communion	Morning Prayer	Evening Prayer
Thursday	**19 October** Henry Martyn, translator, missionary, 1812 (see p.88)	Gw	Romans 3.21–30 Psalm 130 Luke 11.47–end	Psalms 113, 115 Ecclesiasticus 24.23–end or Ezekiel 34.1–16 John 13.31–end	Psalms 114, 116, 117 2 Kings 19.1–19 Philippians 2.14–end
Friday	**20 October**	G	Romans 4.1–8 Psalm 32 Luke 12.1–7	Psalm 139 Ecclesiasticus 27.30—28.9 or Ezekiel 34.17–end John 14.1–14	Psalms 130, 131, 137 2 Kings 19.20–36 Philippians 3.1—4.1
Saturday	**21 October**	G	Romans 4.13, 16–18 Psalm 105.6–10, 41–44	Psalms 120, 121, 122 Ecclesiasticus 28.14–end	Psalm 118 2 Kings 20

	Principal Service	3rd Service	2nd Service
Sunday 22 October G **20th Sunday after Trinity** Proper 24	*Continuous:* Exodus 33.12–end Psalm 99 *Related:* Isaiah 45.1–7 Psalm 96.1–9 [10–13] 1 Thessalonians 1.1–10 Matthew 22.15–22	Psalms 145, 149 Isaiah 54.1–14 Luke 13.31–end	Psalms 142 [143.1–11] Proverbs 4.1–18 1 John 3.16—4.6 HC Mark 10.35–45

	Holy Communion	Morning Prayer	Evening Prayer
Monday 23 October G DEL week 29	Romans 4.20–end *Canticle:* Benedictus 1–6 Luke 12.13–21	Psalms 123, 124, 125, **126** Ecclesiasticus 31.1–11 or Ezekiel 37.1–14 John 15.1–11	Psalms **127**, 128, 129 2 Kings 21.1–18 1 Timothy 1.1–17
Tuesday 24 October G	Romans 5.12, 15, 17–end Psalm 40.7–12 Luke 12.35–38	Psalms **132**, 133 Ecclesiasticus **34.9**–end or Ezekiel 37.15–end John 15.12–17	Psalms (134,) **135** 2 Kings 22.1—23.3 1 Timothy 1.18—end of 2
Wednesday 25 October G *Crispin and Crispinian, martyrs, c.287*	Romans 6.12–18 Psalm 124 Luke 12.39–48	Psalm 119.**153–end** Ecclesiasticus 35 or Ezekiel 39.21–end John 15.18–end	Psalm 136 2 Kings 23.4–25 1 Timothy 3
Thursday 26 October Gw *Alfred, king, scholar, 899* (see p.89) *Cedd, abbot, bishop, 664*	Romans 6.19–end Psalm 1 Luke 12.49–53	Psalms **143**, 146 Ecclesiasticus 37.7–24 or Ezekiel 43.1–12 John 16.1–15	Psalms 138, 140, 141 2 Kings 23.36—24.17 1 Timothy 4
Friday 27 October G	Romans 7.18–end Psalm 119.33–40 Luke 12.54–end	Psalms 142, **144** Ecclesiasticus 38.1–14 or Ezekiel 44.4–16 John 16.16–22	Psalm **145** 2 Kings 24.18—25.12 1 Timothy 5.1–16 *or:* 1st EP of Simon and Jude, Apostles: Psalms 124, 125, 126; Deuteronomy 32.1–4; John 14.15–26

	Principal Service	3rd Service	2nd Service
Saturday 28 October R *Simon and Jude, Apostles*	Isaiah 28.14–16 Psalm 119.89–96 Ephesians 2.19–end John 15.17–end	MP Psalms 116, 117 Wisdom 5.1–16 or Isaiah 45.18–end Luke 6.12–16	EP Psalm 119.1–16 1 Maccabees 2.42–66 or Jeremiah 3.11–18 Jude 1–4, 17–end

Last after Trinity

		Principal Service	3rd Service	2nd Service
Sunday	**29 October** **Last Sunday after Trinity** Proper 25	G	*Continuous:* Deuteronomy 34.1–12 Psalm 90.1–6, 13–17 [or 90.1–6] 1 Thessalonians 2.1–8 Matthew 22.34–end *Related:* Leviticus 19.1–2, 15–18 Psalm 1	Psalm 119.137–152 Isaiah 59.9–20 Luke 14.1–14	Psalm 119.89–104 Ecclesiastes 11, 12 2 Timothy 2.1–7 HC Mark 12.28–34
or **Sunday**	**29 October** **Bible Sunday**	G	Nehemiah 8.1–4a [5–6] 8–12 Psalm 119.9–16 Colossians 3.12–17 Matthew 24.30–35	Psalm 119.137–152 Deuteronomy 17.14–15, 18–end John 5.36b–end	Psalm 119.89–104 Isaiah 55.1–11 Luke 4.14–30

or, if the date of dedication of a church is not known, the Dedication Festival (Gold or W) may be celebrated today or on 1 October, or on a suitable date chosen locally (see p.84).

		Holy Communion	Morning Prayer	Evening Prayer
Monday	**30 October** DEL week 30	G	Romans 8.12–17 Psalm 68.1–6, 19 Luke 13.10–17	Psalms 1, 2, 3 Ecclesiasticus 39.1–11 or Ecclesiastes 1 John 17.1–5	Psalms **4**, 7 Judith 4 or Exodus 22.21–27, 23.1–17 1 Timothy 6.1–10
Tuesday	**31 October** *Martin Luther, reformer, 1546*	G	Romans 8.18–25 Psalm 126 Luke 13.18–21	Psalms **5**, 6 (8) Ecclesiasticus 39.13–end or Ecclesiastes 2 John 17.6–19	Psalms **9**, 10* Judith 5.1–6.4 or Exodus 29.38–30.16 1 Timothy 6.11–end or, if All Saints' Day is celebrated on Wednesday 1 November only: **1st EP of All Saints' Day** Psalms 1, 5 Ecclesiasticus 44.1–15 or Isaiah 40.27–end Revelation 19.6–10

All Saints' Day is celebrated on Wednesday 1 November or on Sunday 5 November; if the latter there may be a supplementary celebration on 1 November.
If All Saints' Day is celebrated on Wednesday 1 November:

		Principal Service	3rd Service	2nd Service
Wednesday	**1 November** All Saints' Day	Revelation 7.9–end Psalm 34.1–10 1 John 3.1–3 Matthew 5.1–12	MP Psalms 15, 84, 149 Isaiah 35 Luke 9.18–27	EP Psalms 148, 150 Isaiah 65.17–end Hebrews 11.32—12.2
	Gold or W			

If All Saints' Day is celebrated on Wednesday 1 November in addition to Sunday 5 November:

		Principal Service	3rd Service	2nd Service
Wednesday	**1 November** All Saints' Day	Isaiah 56.3–8 or 2 Esdras 2.42–end Psalm 33.1–5 Hebrews 12.18–24 Matthew 5.1–12	MP Psalms 111, 112, 117 Wisdom 5.1–16 or Jeremiah 31.31–34 2 Corinthians 4.5–12	EP Psalm 145 Isaiah 66.20–23 Colossians 1.9–14
	Gold or W			

		Holy Communion	Morning Prayer	Evening Prayer
Thursday	**2 November** Commemoration of the Faithful Departed (All Souls' Day) *Rp/Gp*	Romans 8.31–end Psalm 109.20–26, 29–30 Luke 13.31–end *Lesser Festival eucharistic lectionary:* Lamentations 3.17–26, 31–33 or Wisdom 3.1–9 Psalm 23 or 27.1–6, 16–end Romans 5.5–11 or 1 Peter 1.3–9 John 5.19–25 or John 6.37–40	Psalms 14, **15**, 16 Ecclesiasticus 43.1–12 or Ecclesiastes 3.16–end of 4 John 18.1–11	Psalm **18*** Judith 7.19–end or Leviticus 9 2 Timothy 1.15—2.13
Friday	**3 November** Richard Hooker, priest, teacher of the faith, 1600 (p.86) *Martin of Porres, friar, 1639* *Rw/Gw*	Romans 9.1–5 Psalm 147.13–end Luke 14.1–6	Psalms 17, **19** Ecclesiasticus 43.13–end or Ecclesiastes 5 John 18.12–27	Psalm **22** Judith 8.9–end or Leviticus 16.2–24 2 Timothy 2.14–end
Saturday	**4 November** *R/G*	Romans 11.1–2, 11–12, 25–29 Psalm 94.14–19 Luke 14.1, 7–11	Psalms 20, 21, **23** Ecclesiasticus 44.1–15 or Ecclesiastes 6 John 18.28–end	Psalms **24**, 25 Judith 9 or Leviticus 17 2 Timothy 3

		Principal Service	3rd Service	2nd Service
Sunday	**5 November** 4th Sunday before Advent *R/G*	Micah 3.5–end Psalm 43 [or 107.1–8] 1 Thessalonians 2.9–13 Matthew 24.1–14	Psalm 33 Isaiah 66.20–23 Ephesians 1.11–end	Psalms 111, 117 Daniel 7.1–18 Luke 6.17–31

All Saints' Day / 4 before Advent

If All Saints' Day is celebrated on Sunday 5 November only:

		Holy Communion	Morning Prayer	Evening Prayer
Wednesday	1 November — G	Romans 8.26–30 Psalm 13 Luke 13.22–30	Psalm 119.1–32 Ecclesiasticus 42.15–end or Ecclesiastes 3.1–15 John 17.20–end	Psalms 11, 12, 13 Judith 6.10—7.7 or Leviticus 8 2 Timothy 1.1–14
Thursday	2 November — Gp Commemoration of the Faithful Departed (All Souls' Day)	Romans 8.31–end Psalm 109.20–26, 29–30 Luke 13.31–end *Lesser Festival eucharistic lectionary:* Lamentations 3.17–26, 31–33 or Wisdom 3.1–9 Psalm 23 or 27.1–6, 16–end Romans 5.5–11 or 1 Peter 1.3–9 John 5.19–25 or John 6.37–40	Psalms 14, 15, 16 Ecclesiasticus 43.1–12 or Ecclesiastes 3.16—end of 4 John 18.1–11	Psalm 18* Judith 7.19–end or Leviticus 9 2 Timothy 1.15—2.13
Friday	3 November — Gw Richard Hooker, priest, teacher of the faith, 1600 (p.86) *Martin of Porres, friar, 1639*	Romans 9.1–5 Psalm 147.13–end Luke 14.1–6	Psalms 17, 19 Ecclesiasticus 43.13–end or Ecclesiastes 5 John 18.12–27	Psalm 22 Judith 8.9–end or Leviticus 16.2–24 2 Timothy 2.14–end
Saturday	4 November — G	Romans 11.1–2, 11–12, 25–29 Psalm 94.14–19 Luke 14.1, 7–11	Psalms 20, 21, 23 Ecclesiasticus 44.1–15 or Ecclesiastes 6 John 18.28–end	**1st EP of All Saints' Day** Psalms 1, 5 Ecclesiasticus 44.1–15 or Isaiah 40.27–end Revelation 19.6–10
		Principal Service	**3rd Service**	**2nd Service**
Sunday	5 November — Gold or W All Saints' Day	Revelation 7.9–end Psalm 34.1–10 1 John 3.1–3 Matthew 5.1–12	MP Psalms 15, 84, 149 Isaiah 35 Luke 9.18–27	EP Psalms 148, 150 Isaiah 65.17–end Hebrews 11.32—12.2

	Holy Communion	Morning Prayer	Evening Prayer
Monday 6 November *R/G* *Leonard, hermit, 6th cent.* *William Temple, archbishop,* *teacher of the faith, 1944* DEL week 31	Romans 11.29–end Psalm 69.31–37 Luke 14.12–14	Psalms **2**, 146 or 27, **30** Isaiah 1.1–20 Matthew 1.18–end	Psalms **92**, 96, 97 or 26, **28**, 29 Daniel 1 Revelation 1
Tuesday 7 November *Rw/Gw* *Willibrord, bishop, 739 (see p.88)*	Romans 12.5–16 Psalm 131 Luke 14.15–24	Psalms **5**, 147.1–12 or 32, **36** Isaiah 1.21–end Matthew 2.1–15	Psalms 98, 99, **100** or 33 Daniel 2.1–24 Revelation 2.1–11
Wednesday 8 November *Rw/Gw* Saints and martyrs of England	Romans 13.8–10 Psalm 112 Luke 14.25–33 *Lesser Festival eucharistic lectionary:* Isaiah 61.4–9 or Ecclesiasticus 44.1–15 Psalm 15 Revelation 19.5–10 John 17.18–23	Psalms **9**, 147.13–end or **34** Isaiah 2.1–11 Matthew 2.16–end	Psalms 111, **112**, 116 or 119.33–**56** Daniel 2.25–end Revelation 2.12–end
Thursday 9 November *R/G* *Margery Kempe, mystic, c.1440*	Romans 14.7–12 Psalm 27.14–end Luke 15.1–10	Psalms 11, **15**, 148 or **37*** Isaiah 2.12–end Matthew 3	Psalm 118 or 39, **40** Daniel 3.1–18 Revelation 3.1–13
Friday 10 November *Rw/Gw* *Leo the Great, bishop,* *teacher of the faith, 461 (see p.86)*	Romans 15.14–21 Psalm 98 Luke 16.1–8	Psalms **16**, 149 or 31 Isaiah 3.1–15 Matthew 4.1–11	Psalms 137, 138, **143** or **35** Daniel 3.19–end Revelation 3.14–end
Saturday 11 November *Rw/Gw* *Martin, bishop, c.397 (see p.87)*	Romans 16.3–9, 16, 22–end Psalm 145.1–7 Luke 16.9–15	Psalms **18.31–end**, 150 or 41, **42**, 43 Isaiah 4.2–5.7 Matthew 4.12–22	Psalm 145 or 45, **46** Daniel 4.1–18 Revelation 4

3 before Advent

		Principal Service	3rd Service	2nd Service
		Holy Communion	Morning Prayer	Evening Prayer
Sunday	**12 November** *R/G* **3rd Sunday before Advent** *Remembrance Sunday*	Wisdom 6.12–16 or Amos 5.18–24 *Canticle:* Wisdom 6.17–20 or Psalm 70 1 Thessalonians 4.13–end Matthew 25.1–13	Psalm 91 Deuteronomy 17.14–end 1 Timothy 2.1–7	Psalms [20] 82 Judges 7.2–22 John 15.9–17
Monday	**13 November** *Rw/Gw* Charles Simeon, priest, evangelical divine, 1836 (see p.87) DEL week 32	Wisdom 1.1–7 or Titus 1.1–9 Psalm 139.1–9 or 24.1–6 Luke 17.1–6	Psalms 19, **20** or **44** Isaiah 5.8–24 Matthew 4.23—5.12	Psalm **34** or **47**, 49 Daniel 4.19–end Revelation 5
Tuesday	**14 November** *R/G* *Samuel Seabury, bishop, 1796*	Wisdom 2.23–3.9 or Titus 2.1–8, 11–14 Psalm 34.1–6 or 37.3–5, 30–32 Luke 17.7–10	Psalms **21**, 24 or **48**, 52 Isaiah 5.25–end Matthew 5.13–20	Psalms 36, **40** or **50** Daniel 5.1–12 Revelation 6
Wednesday	**15 November** *R/G*	Wisdom 6.1–11 or Titus 3.1–7 Psalm 82 or 23 Luke 17.11–19	Psalms **23**, 25 or 1 1**9.57–80** Isaiah 6 Matthew 5.21–37	Psalm 37 or **59**, 60 (67) Daniel 5.13–end Revelation 7.1–4, 9–end
Thursday	**16 November** *Rw/Gw* Margaret, queen, philanthropist, 1093 (see p.89) *Edmund Rich, archbishop, 1240*	Wisdom 7.22–8.1 or Philemon 7–20 Psalm 119.89–96 or 146.4–end Luke 17.20–25	Psalms **26**, 27 or 56, **57** (63*) Isaiah 7.1–17 Matthew 5.38–end	Psalms 42, **43** or 61, **62**, 64 Daniel 6 Revelation 8
Friday	**17 November** *Rw/Gw* Hugh, bishop, 1200 (see p.87)	Wisdom 13.1–9 or 2 John 4–9 Psalm 19.1–4 or 119.1–8 Luke 17.26–end	Psalms 28, **32** or **51**, 54 Isaiah 8.1–15 Matthew 6.1–18	Psalm **31** or **38** Daniel 7.1–14 Revelation 9.1–12
Saturday	**18 November** *Rw/Gw* Elizabeth, princess, philanthropist, 1231 (see p.89)	Wisdom 18.14–16; 19.6–9 or 3 John 5–8 Psalm 105.1–5, 35–42 or 112 Luke 18.1–8	Psalm **33** or **68** Isaiah 8.16—9.7 Matthew 6.19–end	Psalms 84, **86** or 65, **66** Daniel 7.15–end Revelation 9.13–end

		Principal Service	3rd Service	2nd Service
Sunday	**19 November** *R/G* **2nd Sunday before Advent**	Zephaniah 1.7, 12–end Psalm 90.1–8 [9–11], 12 [or 90.1–8] 1 Thessalonians 5.1–11 Matthew 25.14–30	Psalm 98 Daniel 10.19–end Revelation 4	Psalm 89.19–37 [or 89.19–29] 1 Kings 1.15–40 (or 1–40) Revelation 1.4–18 HC Luke 9.1–6
		Holy Communion	*Morning Prayer*	*Evening Prayer*
Monday	**20 November** *R/Gr* Edmund, king, martyr, 870 (see p.85) *Priscilla Lydia Sellon, a restorer of the religious life in the Church of England, 1876* DEL week 33	1 Maccabees 1.10–15, 41–43, 54–57, 62–64 or Revelation 1.1–4, 2.1–5 Psalm 79.1–5 or 1 Luke 18.35–end	Psalms 46, 47 or 71 Isaiah 9.8–10.4 Matthew 7.1–12	Psalms 70, 71 or 72, 75 Daniel 8.1–14 Revelation 10
Tuesday	**21 November** *R/G*	2 Maccabees 6.18–end or Revelation 3.1–6, 14–31 Psalm 11 or 15 Luke 19.1–10	Psalms 48, 52 or 73 Isaiah 10.5–19 Matthew 7.13–end	Psalms 67, 72 or 74 Daniel 8.15–end Revelation 11.1–14
Wednesday	**22 November** *R/G* *Cecilia, martyr, c.230*	2 Maccabees 7.1, 20–31 or Revelation 4 Psalm 116.10–end or 150 Luke 19.11–28	Psalms 56, 57 or 77 Isaiah 10.20–32 Matthew 8.1–13	Psalm 73 or 119.81–104 Daniel 9.1–19 Revelation 11.15–end
Thursday	**23 November** *R/Gr* Clement, bishop, martyr, c.100 (see p.85)	1 Maccabees 2.15–29 or Revelation 5.1–10 Psalm 129 or 149.1–5 Luke 19.41–44	Psalms 61, **62** or **78.1–39* Isaiah 10.33—11.9 Matthew 8.14–22	Psalms 74, **76** or **78.40–end** Daniel 9.20–end Revelation 12
Friday	**24 November** *R/G*	1 Maccabees 4.36–37, 52–59 or Revelation 10.8–11 Psalm 122 or 119.65–72 Luke 19.45–end	Psalms 63, 65 or 55 Isaiah 11.10–end of 12 Matthew 8.23–end	Psalm 77 or 69 Daniel 10.1—11.1 Revelation 13.1–10
Saturday	**25 November** *R/G* *Catherine, martyr, 4th cent.* *Isaac Watts, hymn writer, 1748*	1 Maccabees 6.1–13 or Revelation 11.4–12 Psalm 124 or 144.1–9 Luke 20.27–40	Psalm 78.1–39 or 76, 79 Isaiah 13.1–13 Matthew 9.1–17	Psalm **78.40–end** or 81, **84** Daniel 12 Revelation 13.11–end or: 1st EP of Christ the King: Psalms 99, 100; Isaiah 10.33—11.9; 1 Timothy 6.11–16

Christ the King / Sunday next before Advent

	Principal Service	3rd Service	2nd Service
Sunday **26 November** *R/W* Christ the King *Sunday next before Advent*	Ezekiel 34.11–16, 20–24 Psalm 95.1–7 Ephesians 1.15–end Matthew 25.31–end	MP Psalms 29, 110 Isaiah 4.2—5.7 Luke 19.29–38	EP Psalms 93 [97] 2 Samuel 23.1–7 or 1 Maccabees 2.15–29 Matthew 28.16–end
	Holy Communion	**Morning Prayer**	**Evening Prayer**
Monday **27 November** *R/G* DEL week 34	Daniel 1.1–6, 8–20 *Canticle:* Bless the Lord Luke 21.1–4	Psalms 92, **96** or **80**, 82 Isaiah 14.3–20 Matthew 9.18–34	Psalms **80**, 81 or **85**, 86 Isaiah 40.1–11 Revelation 14.1–13
Tuesday **28 November** *R/G*	Daniel 2.31–45 *Canticle:* Benedicite 1–3 Luke 21.5–11	Psalms **97**, 98, 100 or 87, **89.1–18** Isaiah 17 Matthew 9.35—10.15	Psalms 99, **101** or **89.19–end** Isaiah 40.12–26 Revelation 14.14—end of 15
Wednesday **29 November** *R/G* *Day of Intercession and Thanksgiving for the Missionary Work of the Church*	Daniel 5.1–6, 13–14, 16–17, 23–28 *Canticle:* Benedicite 4–5 Luke 21.12–19	Psalms 110, 111, **112** or **119.105–128** Isaiah 19 Matthew 10.16–33	Psalms 121, **122**, 123, 124 or **91**, 93 Isaiah 40.27—41.7 Revelation 16.1–11 or: 1st EP of Andrew the Apostle: Psalm 48; Isaiah 49.1–9a; 1 Corinthians 4.9–16
	Principal Service	**3rd Service**	**2nd Service**
Thursday **30 November** *R* Andrew the Apostle	Isaiah 52.7–10 Psalm 19.1–6 Romans 10.12–18 Matthew 4.18–22	MP Psalms 47, 147.1–12 Ezekiel 47.1–12 or Ecclesiasticus 14.20–end John 12.20–32	EP Psalms 87, 96 Zechariah 8.20–end John 1.35–42
	Holy Communion	**Morning Prayer**	**Evening Prayer**
Friday **1 December** *R/G* *Charles de Foucauld, hermit, 1916*	Daniel 7.2–14 *Canticle:* Benedicite 8b–10a Luke 21.29–33	Psalm 139 or 88 (95) Isaiah 22.1–14 Matthew 11.2–19	Psalms 146, 147 or **102** Isaiah 41.21—42.9 Revelation 17
Saturday **2 December** *R/G*	Daniel 7.15–27 *Canticle:* Benedicite 10b–end Luke 21.34–36	Psalm 145 or 96, **97**, 100 Isaiah 24 Matthew 11.20–end	Psalms 148, 149, **150** or **104** Isaiah 42.10–17 Revelation 18

This Additional Weekday Lectionary provides two readings for each day of the year, except
for Sundays, Principal Feasts and other Principal Holy Days, Holy Week and Festivals (for
which the readings provided in the main body of this lectionary are used). The readings for
'first evensongs' in the main body of the lectionary are used on the eves of Principal Feasts
and may be used on the eves of Festivals. This lectionary is intended particularly for use in
those places of worship that attract occasional rather than daily worshippers, and can be
used either at Morning or Evening Prayer. Psalmody is not provided and should be taken from
the daily provision earlier in this volume.

		27 November – Advent 1	
Monday	**28 November**	Malachi 3.1–6	Matthew 3.1–6
Tuesday	**29 November**	Zephaniah 3.14–end	I Thessalonians 4.13–end
		or 1st EP of Andrew the Apostle	
Wednesday	**30 November**	Andrew the Apostle – see p.10	
Thursday	**1 December**	Micah 5.2–5a	John 3.16–21
Friday	**2 December**	Isaiah 66.18–end	Luke 13.22–30
Saturday	**3 December**	Micah 7.8–15	Romans 15.30—16.7, 25–end

		4 December – Advent 2	
Monday	**5 December**	Jeremiah 7.1–11	Philippians 4.4–9
Tuesday	**6 December**	Daniel 7.9–14	Matthew 24.15–28
Wednesday	**7 December**	Amos 9.11–end	Romans 13.8–14
Thursday	**8 December**	Jeremiah 23.5–8	Mark 11.1–11
Friday	**9 December**	Jeremiah 33.14–22	Luke 21.25–36
Saturday	**10 December**	Zechariah 14.4–11	Revelation 22.1–7

		11 December – Advent 3	
Monday	**12 December**	Isaiah 40.1–11	Matthew 3.1–12
Tuesday	**13 December**	Lamentations 3.22–33	I Corinthians 1.1–9
Wednesday	**14 December**	Joel 3.9–16	Matthew 24.29–35
Thursday	**15 December**	Isaiah 62	I Thessalonians 3.6–13
Friday	**16 December**	Isaiah 2.1–5	Acts 11.1–18
Saturday	**17 December**	Ecclesiasticus 24.1–9	I Corinthians 2.1–13
		or Proverbs 8.22–31	

		18 December – Advent 4	
Monday	**19 December**	Isaiah 11.1–9	Romans 15.7–13
Tuesday	**20 December**	Isaiah 22.21–23	Revelation 3.7–13
Wednesday	**21 December**	Numbers 24.15b–19	Revelation 22.10–21
Thursday	**22 December**	Jeremiah 30.7–11a	Acts 4.1–12
Friday	**23 December**	Isaiah 7.10–15	Matthew 1.18–23
Saturday	**24 December**	At Evening Prayer the readings for Christmas Eve are used.	
		At other services, the following readings are used:	
		Isaiah 29.13–18	I John 4.7–16

		25 December – Christmas Day	
Monday	**26 December**	Stephen, deacon, first martyr – see p.14	
Tuesday	**27 December**	John, Apostle and Evangelist – see p.14	
Wednesday	**28 December**	The Holy Innocents – see p.14	
Thursday	**29 December**	Micah 1.1–4; 2.12–13	Luke 2.1–7
Friday	**30 December**	Isaiah 9.2–7	John 8.12–20
Saturday	**31 December**	Ecclesiastes 3.1–13	Revelation 21.1–8
		or 1st EP of Naming and Circumcision	
		of Jesus	

		If **The Epiphany** is celebrated on Wednesday 6 January:	
Monday	**2 January**	Isaiah 66.6–14	Matthew 12.46–50
		or Naming and Circumcision of Jesus	
		(transferred from 1 January) – see p.15	
Tuesday	**3 January**	Deuteronomy 6.4–15	John 10.31–end
Wednesday	**4 January**	Isaiah 63.7–16	Galatians 3.23—4.7
Thursday	**5 January**	At Evening Prayer the readings for the Eve of the Epiphany are used.	
		At other services, the following readings are used:	
		Isaiah 12	2 Corinthians 2.12–end
Friday	**6 January**	The Epiphany – see p.16	
Saturday	**7 January**	At Evening Prayer the readings for the Eve of the Baptism of Christ	
		are used. At other services, the following readings are used:	
		Genesis 25.19–end	Ephesians 1.1–6
Sunday	**8 January**	The Baptism of Christ – see p.16	
Monday	**9 January**	Isaiah 41.14–20	John 1.29–34

		If, for pastoral reasons, The Epiphany is celebrated on Sunday 8 January:	
Monday	**2 January**	Isaiah 66.6–14	Matthew 12.46–50
		or Naming and Circumcision of Jesus	
		(transferred from 1 January) –see p.15	
Tuesday	**3 January**	Deuteronomy 6.4–15	John 10.31–end
Wednesday	**4 January**	Isaiah 63.7–16	Galatians 3.23—4.7
Thursday	**5 January**	Isaiah 12	2 Corinthians 2.12–end
Friday	**6 January**	Genesis 25.19–end	Ephesians 1.1–6
Saturday	**7 January**	At Evening Prayer the readings for the Eve of the Epiphany are used.	
		At other services, the following readings are used:	
		Joel 2.28–end	Ephesians 1.7–14
Sunday	**8 January**	The Epiphany – see p.17	
Monday	**9 January**	The Baptism of Christ – see p.17	

Tuesday	**10 January**	Exodus 17.1–7	Acts 8.26–end
Wednesday	**11 January**	Exodus 15.1–19	Colossians 2.8–15
Thursday	**12 January**	Zechariah 6.9–15	1 Peter 2.4–10
Friday	**13 January**	Isaiah 51.7–16	Galatians 6.14–18
Saturday	**14 January**	Leviticus 16.11–22	Hebrews 10.19–25

Monday	**16 January**	1 Kings 17.8–16	Mark 8.1–10
Tuesday	**17 January**	1 Kings 19.1–9a	Mark 1.9–15
Wednesday	**18 January**	1 Kings 19.9b–18	Mark 9.2–13
Thursday	**19 January**	Leviticus 11.1–8, 13–19, 41–45	Acts 10.9–16
Friday	**20 January**	Isaiah 49.8–13	Acts 10.34–43
Saturday	**21 January**	Genesis 35.1–15	Acts 10.44–end

Monday	**23 January**	Ezekiel 37.15–end	John 17.1–19
Tuesday	**24 January**	Ezekiel 20.39–44	John 17.20–end
		or 1st EP of the Conversion of Paul	
Wednesday	**25 January**	Conversion of Paul – see p.20	
Thursday	**26 January**	Deuteronomy 26.16–end	Romans 14.1–9
Friday	**27 January**	Leviticus 19.9–28	Romans 15.1–7
Saturday	**28 January**	Jeremiah 33.1–11	1 Peter 5.5b–end
		If, for pastoral reasons, the Presentation of Christ is celebrated on Sunday 29 January, the readings for the Eve of the Presentation are used at Evening Prayer.	

Monday	**30 January**	Jonah 3	2 Corinthians 5.11–21
Tuesday	**31 January**	Proverbs 4.10–end	Matthew 5.13–20
Wednesday	**1 February**	Isaiah 61.1–9	Luke 7.18–30

If the Presentation of Christ *is celebrated on Thursday 2 February, the readings for the Eve of the Presentation are used at Evening Prayer.*

Thursday	**2 February**	Presentation of Christ – see p.22	

or, if, for pastoral reasons, the Presentation of Christ *is celebrated on Sunday 29 January:*

		Isaiah 52.1–12	Matthew 10.1–15
Friday	**3 February**	Isaiah 56.1–8	Matthew 28.16–end
Saturday	**4 February**	Habakkuk 2.1–4	Revelation 14.1–7

Monday	**6 February**	Exodus 23.1–13	James 2.1–13
Tuesday	**7 February**	Deuteronomy 10.12–end	Hebrews 13.1–16
Wednesday	**8 February**	Isaiah 58.6–end	Matthew 25.31–end
Thursday	**9 February**	Isaiah 42.1–9	Luke 4.14–21
Friday	**10 February**	Amos 5.6–15	Ephesians 4.25–end
Saturday	**11 February**	Amos 5.18–24	John 2.13–22

Monday	**13 February**	Isaiah 61.1–9	Mark 6.1–13
Tuesday	**14 February**	Isaiah 52.1–10	Romans 10.5–21
Wednesday	**15 February**	Isaiah 52.13—53.6	Romans 15.14–21
Thursday	**16 February**	Isaiah 53.4–12	2 Corinthians 4.1–10
Friday	**17 February**	Zechariah 8.16–end	Matthew 10.1–15
Saturday	**18 February**	Jeremiah 1.4–10	Matthew 10.16–22

Monday	**20 February**	2 Kings 2.13–22	3 John
Tuesday	**21 February**	Judges 14.5–17	Revelation 10.4–11
Wednesday	**22 February**	Ash Wednesday – see p.26	
Thursday	**23 February**	Genesis 2.7–end	Hebrews 2.5–end
Friday	**24 February**	Genesis 4.1–12	Hebrews 4.12–end
Saturday	**25 February**	2 Kings 22.11–end	Hebrews 5.1–10

Monday	**27 February**	Genesis 6.11–end; 7.11–16	Luke 4.14–21
Tuesday	**28 February**	Deuteronomy 31.7–13	1 John 3.1–10
Wednesday	**1 March**	Genesis 11.1–9	Matthew 24.15–28
Thursday	**2 March**	Genesis 13.1–13	1 Peter 2.13–end
Friday	**3 March**	Genesis 21.1–8	Luke 9.18–27
Saturday	**4 March**	Genesis 32.22–32	2 Peter 1.10–end

Monday	**6 March**	1 Chronicles 21.1–17	1 John 2.1–8
Tuesday	**7 March**	Zechariah 3	2 Peter 2.1–10a
Wednesday	**8 March**	Job 1.1–22	Luke 21.34—22.6
Thursday	**9 March**	2 Chronicles 29.1–11	Mark 11.15–19
Friday	**10 March**	Exodus 19.1–9a	1 Peter 1.1–9
Saturday	**11 March**	Exodus 19.9b–19	Acts 7.44–50

Monday	**13 March**	Joshua 4.1–13	Luke 9.1–11
Tuesday	**14 March**	Exodus 15.22–27	Hebrews 10.32–end
Wednesday	**15 March**	Genesis 9.8–17	1 Peter 3.18–end
Thursday	**16 March**	Daniel 12.5–end	Mark 13.21–end
Friday	**17 March**	Numbers 20.1–13	1 Corinthians 10.23–end
Saturday	**18 March**	Isaiah 43.14–end	Hebrews 3.1–15

Monday	**20 March**	Joseph of Nazareth (transferred from 19 March) – see p.30	
Tuesday	**21 March**	Jeremiah 13.12–19	Acts 13.26–35
Wednesday	**22 March**	Jeremiah 13.20–27	1 Peter 1.17—2.3
Thursday	**23 March**	Jeremiah 22.11–19	Luke 11.37–52
Friday	**24 March**	*At Evening Prayer, the readings for the Eve of the Annunciation are used.*	
		At other services, the following readings are used:	
		Jeremiah 17.1–4	Luke 6.17–26
Saturday	**25 March**	Annunciation of Our Lord to the	
		Blessed Virgin Mary – see p.30	

Monday	**27 March**	Joel 2.12–17	2 John
Tuesday	**28 March**	Isaiah 58.1–14	Mark 10.32–45
Wednesday	**29 March**	Job 36.1–12	John 14.1–14
Thursday	**30 March**	Jeremiah 9.17–22	Luke 13.31–35
Friday	**31 March**	Lamentations 5.1–3, 19–22	John 12.20–26
Saturday	**1 April**	Job 17.6–end	John 12.27–36

From the Monday of Holy Week until Easter Eve the seasonal lectionary is used: see pp.32–33.

Monday	**10 April**	Isaiah 54.1–14	Romans 1.1–7
Tuesday	**11 April**	Isaiah 51.1–11	John 5.19–29
Wednesday	**12 April**	Isaiah 26.1–19	John 20.1–10
Thursday	**13 April**	Isaiah 43.14–21	Revelation 1.4–end
Friday	**14 April**	Isaiah 42.10–17	1 Thessalonians 5.1–11
Saturday	**15 April**	Job 14.1–14	John 21.1–14

Monday	**17 April**	Ezekiel 1.22–end	Revelation 4
Tuesday	**18 April**	Proverbs 8.1–11	Acts 16.6–15
Wednesday	**19 April**	Hosea 5.15—6.6	1 Corinthians 15.1–11
Thursday	**20 April**	Jonah 2	Mark 4.35–end
Friday	**21 April**	Genesis 6.9–end	1 Peter 3.8–end
Saturday	**22 April**	1 Samuel 2.1–8	Matthew 28.8–15

Monday	**24 April**	George, Martyr, Patron of England	
		(transferred from 23 April) – see p.36	
Tuesday	**25 April**	Mark the Evangelist – see p.36	
Wednesday	**26 April**	Genesis 3.8–21	1 Corinthians 15.12–28
Thursday	**27 April**	Isaiah 33.13–22	Mark 6.47–end
Friday	**28 April**	Nehemiah 9.6–17	Romans 5.12–end
Saturday	**29 April**	Isaiah 61.10—62.5	Luke 24.1–12

Monday	**1 May**	Philip and James, Apostles – see p.37	
Tuesday	**2 May**	Job 31.13–23	Matthew 7.1–12
Wednesday	**3 May**	Genesis 2.4b–9	1 Corinthians 15.35–49
Thursday	**4 May**	Proverbs 28.3–end	Mark 10.17–31
Friday	**5 May**	Ecclesiastes 12.1–8	Romans 6.1–11
Saturday	**6 May**	1 Chronicles 29.10–13	Luke 24.13–35

Monday	**8 May**	Genesis 15.1–18	Romans 4.13–end
Tuesday	**9 May**	Deuteronomy 8.1–10	Matthew 6.19–end
Wednesday	**10 May**	Hosea 13.4–14	1 Corinthians 15.50–end
Thursday	**11 May**	Exodus 3.1–15	Mark 12.18–27
Friday	**12 May**	Ezekiel 36.33–end	Romans 8.1–11
Saturday	**13 May**	Isaiah 38.9–20	Luke 24.33–end

Monday	**15 May**	Matthias the Apostle (transferred from 14 May) – see p.39	
Tuesday	**16 May**	Isaiah 32.12–end	Romans 5.1–11
Wednesday	**17 May**	At Evening Prayer, the readings for the Eve of Ascension Day are used.	
		At other services, the following readings are used:	
		Isaiah 43.1–13	Titus 2.11–3.8
Thursday	**18 May**	Ascension Day – see p.40	
Friday	**19 May**	Exodus 35.30—36.1	Galatians 5.13–end
Saturday	**20 May**	Numbers 11.16–17, 24–29	1 Corinthians 2

Monday	**22 May**	Numbers 27.15–end	1 Corinthians 3
Tuesday	**23 May**	1 Samuel 10.1–10	1 Corinthians 12.1–13
Wednesday	**24 May**	1 Kings 19.1–18	Matthew 3.13–end
Thursday	**25 May**	Ezekiel 11.14–20	Matthew 9.35—10.20
Friday	**26 May**	Ezekiel 36.22–28	Matthew 12.22–32
Saturday	**27 May**	At Evening Prayer, the readings for the Eve of Pentecost are used.	
		At other services, the following readings are used:	
		Micah 3.1–8	Ephesians 6.10–20

Monday	**29 May**	Genesis 12.1–9	Romans 4.13–end
Tuesday	**30 May**	Genesis 13.1–12	Romans 12.9–end
		or 1st EP of the Visit of the Blessed Virgin Mary to Elizabeth	
Wednesday	**31 May**	Visit of the Blessed Virgin Mary to Elizabeth – see p.42	
Thursday	**1 June**	Genesis 22.1–18	Hebrews 11.8–19
Friday	**2 June**	Isaiah 51.1–8	John 8.48–end
Saturday	**3 June**	At Evening Prayer, the readings for the Eve of Trinity Sunday are used.	
		At other services, the following readings are used:	
		Ecclesiasticus 44.19–23	James 2.14–26
		or Joshua 2.1–15	

Monday	**5 June**	Exodus 2.1–10	Hebrews 11.23–31
Tuesday	**6 June**	Exodus 2.11–end	Acts 7.17–29
Wednesday	**7 June**	Exodus 3.1–12	Acts 7.30–38
		or 1st EP of Corpus Christi	
Thursday	**8 June**	Day of Thanksgiving for the Institution of the Holy Communion (Corpus Christi) – see p.43	
		or, where Corpus Christi is celebrated as a Lesser Festival:	
		Exodus 6.1–13	John 9.24–38
Friday	**9 June**	Exodus 34.1–10	Mark 7.1–13
Saturday	**10 June**	Exodus 34.27–end	2 Corinthians 3.7–end

Monday	**12 June**	Genesis 37.1–11	Romans 12.9–21
		or, Barnabas the Apostle (transferred from 11 June) – see p.45	
Tuesday	**13 June**	Genesis 41.15–40	Mark 13.1–13
Wednesday	**14 June**	Genesis 42.17–end	Matthew 18.1–14
Thursday	**15 June**	Genesis 45.1–15	Acts 7.9–16
Friday	**16 June**	Genesis 47.1–12	1 Thessalonians 5.12–end
Saturday	**17 June**	Genesis 50.4–21	Luke 15.11–end

Monday	**19 June**	Isaiah 32	James 3.13–end
Tuesday	**20 June**	Proverbs 3.1–18	Matthew 5.1–12
Wednesday	**21 June**	Judges 6.1–16	Matthew 5.13–24
Thursday	**22 June**	Jeremiah 6.9–15	1 Timothy 2.1–6
Friday	**23 June**	1 Samuel 16.14–end	John 14.15–end
		or 1st EP of Birth of John the Baptist	
Saturday	**24 June**	Birth of John the Baptist – see p.47	

	25 June – Trinity 3		
Monday	**26 June**	Exodus 13.13b–end	Luke 15.1–10
Tuesday	**27 June**	Proverbs 1.20–end	James 5.13–end
Wednesday	**28 June**	Isaiah 5.8–24	James 1.17–25
		or 1st EP of Peter and Paul, Apostles (*or* Peter the Apostle)	
Thursday	**29 June**	Peter and Paul, Apostles *or* Peter the Apostle – see p.48	
Friday	**30 June**	Jeremiah 15.15–end	Luke 16.19–31
Saturday	**1 July**	Isaiah 25.1–9	Acts 2.22–33
	2 July – Trinity 4		
Monday	**3 July**	Thomas the Apostle – see p.49	
Tuesday	**4 July**	Proverbs 6.6–19	Luke 4.1–14
Wednesday	**5 July**	Isaiah 24.1–15	1 Corinthians 6.1–11
Thursday	**6 July**	Job 7	Matthew 7 21–29
Friday	**7 July**	Jeremiah 20.7–end	Matthew 27.27–44
Saturday	**8 July**	Job 28	Hebrews 11.32—12.2
	9 July – Trinity 5		
Monday	**10 July**	Exodus 32.1–14	Colossians 3.1–11
Tuesday	**11 July**	Proverbs 9.1–12	2 Thessalonians 2.13—3.5
Wednesday	**12 July**	Isaiah 26.1–9	Romans 8.12–27
Thursday	**13 July**	Jeremiah 8.18—9.6	John 13.21–35
Friday	**14 July**	2 Samuel 5.1–12	Matthew 27.45–56
Saturday	**15 July**	Hosea 11.1–11	Matthew 28.1–7
	16 July – Trinity 6		
Monday	**17 July**	Exodus 40.1–16	Luke 14.15–24
Tuesday	**18 July**	Proverbs 11.1–12	Mark 12.38–44
Wednesday	**19 July**	Isaiah 33.2–10	Philippians 1.1–11
Thursday	**20 July**	Job 38	Luke 18.1–14
Friday	**21 July**	Job 42.1–6	John 3.1–15
		or 1st EP of Mary Magdalene	
Saturday	**22 July**	Mary Magdalene – see p.51	
	23 July – Trinity 7		
Monday	**24 July**	Numbers 23.1–12	1 Corinthians 1.10–17
		or 1st EP of James the Apostle	
Tuesday	**25 July**	James the Apostle – see p.52	
Wednesday	**26 July**	Isaiah 49.8–13	2 Corinthians 8.1–11
Thursday	**27 July**	Hosea 14	John 15.1–17
Friday	**28 July**	2 Samuel 18.18–end	Matthew 27.57–66
Saturday	**29 July**	Isaiah 55.1–7	Mark 16.1–8
	30 July – Trinity 8		
Monday	**31 July**	Joel 3.16–21	Mark 4.21–34
Tuesday	**1 August**	Proverbs 12.13–end	John 1.43–51
Wednesday	**2 August**	Isaiah 55.8–end	2 Timothy 2.8–19
Thursday	**3 August**	Isaiah 38.1–8	Mark 5.21–43
Friday	**4 August**	Jeremiah 14.1–9	Luke 8.4–15
Saturday	**5 August**	Ecclesiastes 5.10–19	1 Timothy 6.6–16
	6 August – Transfiguration / Trinity 9		
Monday	**7 August**	Joshua 1.1–9	1 Corinthians 9.19–end
		or The Transfiguration of Our Lord	
		(transferred from 6 August) – see p.55	
Tuesday	**8 August**	Proverbs 15.1–11	Galatians 2.15–end
Wednesday	**9 August**	Isaiah 49.1–7	1 John 1
Thursday	**10 August**	Proverbs 27.1–12	John 15.12–27
Friday	**11 August**	Isaiah 59.8–end	Mark 15.6–20
Saturday	**12 August**	Zechariah 7.8—8.8	Luke 20.27–40

Monday	**14 August**	Judges 13.1–23	Luke 10.38–42
		or 1st EP of the Blessed Virgin Mary	
Tuesday	**15 August**	The Blessed Virgin Mary – see p.57	
Wednesday	**16 August**	Isaiah 45.1–7	Ephesians 4.1–16
Thursday	**17 August**	Jeremiah 16.1–15	Luke 12.35–48
Friday	**18 August**	Jeremiah 18.1–11	Hebrews 1.1–9
Saturday	**19 August**	Jeremiah 26.1–19	Ephesians 3.1–13

Monday	**21 August**	Ruth 2.1–13	Luke 10.25–37
Tuesday	**22 August**	Proverbs 16.1–11	Philippians 3.4b–end
Wednesday	**23 August**	Deuteronomy 11.1–21	2 Corinthians 9.6–end
		or 1st EP of Bartholomew the Apostle	
Thursday	**24 August**	Bartholomew the Apostle – see p.58	
Friday	**25 August**	Obadiah 1–10	John 19.1–16
Saturday	**26 August**	2 Kings 2.11–14	Luke 24.36–end

Monday	**28 August**	1 Samuel 17.32–50	Matthew 8.14–22
Tuesday	**29 August**	Proverbs 17.1–15	Luke 7.1–17
Wednesday	**30 August**	Jeremiah 5.20–end	2 Peter 3.8–end
Thursday	**31 August**	Daniel 2.1–23	Luke 10.1–20
Friday	**1 September**	Daniel 3.1–28	Revelation 15
Saturday	**2 September**	Daniel 6	Philippians 2.14–24

Monday	**4 September**	2 Samuel 7.4–17	2 Corinthians 5.1–10
Tuesday	**5 September**	Proverbs 18.10–21	Romans 14.10–end
Wednesday	**6 September**	Judges 4.1–10	Romans 1.8–17
Thursday	**7 September**	Isaiah 49.14–end	John 16.16–24
Friday	**8 September**	Job 9.1–24	Mark 15.21–32
Saturday	**9 September**	Exodus 19.1–9	John 20.11–18

Monday	**11 September**	Haggai 1	Mark 7.9–23
Tuesday	**12 September**	Proverbs 21.1–18	Mark 6.30–44
Wednesday	**13 September**	Hosea 11.1–11	1 John 4.9–end
		or 1st EP of Holy Cross Day	
Thursday	**14 September**	Holy Cross Day – see p.61	
Friday	**15 September**	2 Kings 19.4–18	1 Thessalonians 3
Saturday	**16 September**	Ecclesiasticus 4.11–28	2 Timothy 3.10–end
		or Deuteronomy 29.2–15	

Monday	**18 September**	Wisdom 6.12–21 or Job 12.1–16	Matthew 15.1–9
Tuesday	**19 September**	Proverbs 8.1–11	Luke 6.39–end
Wednesday	**20 September**	Proverbs 2.1–15	Colossians 1.9–20
		or 1st EP of Matthew, Apostle and Evangelist	
Thursday	**21 September**	Matthew, Apostle and Evangelist – see p.62	
Friday	**22 September**	Ecclesiasticus 1.1–20	1 Corinthians 1.18–end
		or Deuteronomy 7.7–16	
Saturday	**23 September**	Wisdom 9.1–12 or Jeremiah 1.4–10	Luke 2.41–end

Monday	**25 September**	Genesis 21.1–13	Luke 1.26–38
Tuesday	**26 September**	Ruth 4.7–17	Luke 2.25–38
Wednesday	**27 September**	2 Kings 4.1–7	John 2.1–11
Thursday	**28 September**	2 Kings 4.25b–37	Mark 3.19b–35
		or 1st EP of Michael and All Angels	
Friday	**29 September**	Michael and All Angels – see p.63	
Saturday	**30 September**	Exodus 15.19–27	Acts 1.6–14

Monday	**2 October**	Exodus 19.16–end	Hebrews 12.18–end
Tuesday	**3 October**	I Chronicles 16.1–13	Revelation 11.15–end
Wednesday	**4 October**	I Chronicles 29.10–19	Colossians 3.12–17
Thursday	**5 October**	Nehemiah 8.1–12	I Corinthians 14.1–12
Friday	**6 October**	Isaiah 1.10–17	Mark 12.28–34
Saturday	**7 October**	Daniel 6.6–23	Revelation 12.7–12

Monday	**9 October**	2 Samuel 22.4–7, 17–20	Hebrews 7.26—8.6
Tuesday	**10 October**	Proverbs 22.17–end	2 Corinthians 12.1–10
Wednesday	**11 October**	Hosea 14	James 2.14–26
Thursday	**12 October**	Isaiah 24.1–15	John 16.25–33
Friday	**13 October**	Jeremiah 14.1–9	Luke 23.44–56
Saturday	**14 October**	Zechariah 8.14–end	John 20.19–end

Monday	**16 October**	I Kings 3.3–14	I Timothy 3.14—4.8
Tuesday	**17 October**	Proverbs 27.11–end	Galatians 6.1–10
		or 1st EP of Luke the Evangelist	
Wednesday	**18 October**	Luke the Evangelist – see p.66	
Thursday	**19 October**	Ecclesiasticus 18.1–14 or Job 26	I Corinthians 11.17–end
Friday	**20 October**	Ecclesiasticus 28.2–12 or Job 19.21–end	Mark 15.33–47
Saturday	**21 October**	Isaiah 44.21–end	John 21.15–end

Monday	**23 October**	I Kings 6.2–10	John 12.1–11
Tuesday	**24 October**	Proverbs 31.10–end	Luke 10.38–42
Wednesday	**25 October**	Jonah 1	Luke 5.1–11
Thursday	**26 October**	Exodus 12.1–20	I Thessalonians 4.1–12
Friday	**27 October**	Isaiah 64	Matthew 27.45–56
		or 1st EP of Simon and Jude, Apostles	
Saturday	**28 October**	Simon and Jude, Apostles – see p.67	

Monday	**30 October**	Isaiah 42.14–21	Luke 1.5–25
Tuesday	**31 October**	I Samuel 4.12–end	Luke 1.57–80
		or 1st EP of All Saints' Day, if All Saints' Day is celebrated on	
		1 November	
Wednesday	**1 November**	All Saints' Day – see p.69	
		or, if All Saints' Day is celebrated on Sunday 5 November only,	
		the following readings are used:	
		Baruch 5 or Haggai 1.1–11	Mark 1.1–11
Thursday	**2 November**	Isaiah 35	Matthew 11.2–19
Friday	**3 November**	2 Samuel 11.1–17	Matthew 14.1–12
Saturday	**4 November**	Isaiah 43.15–21	Acts 19.1–10
		or 1st EP of All Saints' Day, if All Saints' Day is celebrated on	
		5 November	

Monday	**6 November**	Esther 3.1–11; 4.7–17	Matthew 18.1–10
Tuesday	**7 November**	Ezekiel 18.21–end	Matthew 18.12–20
Wednesday	**8 November**	Proverbs 3.27–end	Matthew 18.21–end
Thursday	**9 November**	Exodus 23.1–9	Matthew 19.1–15
Friday	**10 November**	Proverbs 3.13–18	Matthew 19.16–end
Saturday	**11 November**	Deuteronomy 28.1–6	Matthew 20.1–16

Monday	**13 November**	Isaiah 40.21–end	Romans 11.25–end
Tuesday	**14 November**	Ezekiel 34.20–end	John 10.1–18
Wednesday	**15 November**	Leviticus 26.3–13	Titus 2.1–10
Thursday	**16 November**	Hosea 6.1–6	Matthew 9.9–13
Friday	**17 November**	Malachi 4	John 4.5–26
Saturday	**18 November**	Micah 6.6–8	Colossians 3.12–17

Monday	**20 November**	Micah 7.1–7	Matthew 10.24–39
Tuesday	**21 November**	Habakkuk 3.1–19a	1 Corinthians 4.9–16
Wednesday	**22 November**	Zechariah 8.1–13	Mark 13.3–8
Thursday	**23 November**	Zechariah 10.6–end	1 Peter 5.1–11
Friday	**24 November**	Micah 4.1–5	Luke 9.28–36
Saturday	**25 November**	At Evening Prayer the readings for the Eve of Christ the King are used. At other services, the following readings are used:	
		Exodus 16.1–21	John 6.3–15

Monday	**27 November**	Jeremiah 30.1–3, 10–17	Romans 12.9–21
Tuesday	**28 November**	Jeremiah 30.18–24	John 10.22–30
Wednesday	**29 November**	Jeremiah 31.1–9	Matthew 15.21–31
		or 1st EP of Andrew the Apostle	
Thursday	**30 November**	Andrew the Apostle – see p.74	
Friday	**1 December**	Jeremiah 31.31–37	Hebrews 10.11–18
Saturday	**2 December**	Isaiah 51.17—52.2	Ephesians 5.1–20

¶ Collects and Post Communions

All the contemporary language Collects and Post Communions, including the Additional Collects, may be found in *Common Worship: Collects and Post Communions* (Church House Publishing: London, 2004). The Additional Collects are also published separately.

The contemporary language Collects and Post Communions all appear in *Times and Seasons President's Edition for Holy Communion*. Apart from the Additional Collects, they appear in the other Common Worship volumes as follows:

¶ President's edition: all Collects and Post Communions;
¶ *Daily Prayer*: all Collects;
¶ main volume: Collects and Post Communions for Sundays, Principal Feasts and Holy Days and Festivals;
¶ *Festivals*: Collects and Post Communions for Festivals, Lesser Festivals, Common of the Saints and Special Occasions.

The traditional-language Collects and Post Communions all appear in the president's edition. They appear in other publications as follows:

¶ main volume: Collects and Post Communions for Sundays, Principal Feasts and Holy Days and Festivals;
¶ separate booklet: Collects and Post Communions for Lesser Festivals, Common of the Saints and Special Occasions.

¶ Lectionary for Dedication Festival

If date not known, observe on the first Sunday in October or Last Sunday after Trinity.

Evening Prayer on the Eve	Psalm 24
	2 Chronicles 7.11–16
	John 4.19–29

Dedication Festival — *Gold or White*

	Principal Service	3rd Service	2nd Service	Psalmody
Year A	1 Kings 8.22–30 or Revelation 21.9–14 Psalm 122 Hebrews 12.18–24 Matthew 21.12–16	Haggai 2.6–9 Hebrews 10.19–25	Jeremiah 7.1–11 1 Corinthians 3.9–17 *HC* Luke 19.1–10	*MP* 48, 150 *EP* 132
Year B	Genesis 28.11–18 or Revelation 21.9–14 Psalm 122 1 Peter 2.1–10 John 10.22–29	Haggai 2.6–9 Hebrews 10.19–25	Jeremiah 7.1–11 Luke 19.1–10	*MP* 48, 150 *EP* 132
Year C	1 Chronicles 29.6–19 Psalm 122 Ephesians 2.19–end John 2.13–22	Haggai 2.6–9 Hebrews 10.19–25	Jeremiah 7.1–11 Luke 19.1–10	*MP* 48, 150 *EP* 132

The Blessed Virgin Mary

Genesis 3.8–15, 20; Isaiah 7.10–14; Micah 5.1–4
Psalms 45.10–17; 113; 131
Acts 1.12–14; Romans 8.18–30; Galatians 4.4–7
Luke 1.26–38; *or* 1.39–47; John 19.25–27

Martyrs

2 Chronicles 24.17–21; Isaiah 43.1–7; Jeremiah 11.18–20; Wisdom 4.10–15
Psalms 3; 11; 31.1–5; 44.18–24; 126
Romans 8.35–end; 2 Corinthians 4.7–15; 2 Timothy 2.3–7 [8–13]; Hebrews 11.32–end;
    1 Peter 4.12–end; Revelation 12.10–12a
Matthew 10.16–22; *or* 10.28–39; *or* 16.24–26; John 12.24–26; *or* 15.18–21

Agnes (21 Jan): *also* Revelation 7.13–end
Alban (22 June): *especially* 2 Timothy 2.3–13; John 12.24–26
Alphege (19 Apr): *also* Hebrews 5.1–4
Boniface (5 June): *also* Acts 20.24–28
Charles (30 Jan): *also* Ecclesiasticus 2.12–end; 1 Timothy 6.12–16
Clement (23 Nov): *also* Philippians 3.17—4.3; Matthew 16.13–19
Cyprian (15 Sept): *especially* 1 Peter 4.12–end; *also* Matthew 18.18–22
Edmund (20 Nov): *also* Proverbs 20.28; 21.1–4, 7
Ignatius (17 Oct): *also* Philippians 3.7–12; John 6.52–58
James Hannington (29 Oct): *especially* Matthew 10.28–39
Janani Luwum (17 Feb): *also* Ecclesiasticus 4.20–28; John 12.24–32
John Coleridge Patteson (20 Sept): *especially* 2 Chronicles 24.17–21; *also* Acts 7.55–end
Justin (1 June): *especially* John 15.18–21; *also* 1 Maccabees 2.15–22; 1 Corinthians 1.18–25
Laurence (10 Aug): *also* 2 Corinthians 9.6–10
Lucy (13 Dec): *also* Wisdom 3.1–7; 2 Corinthians 4.6–15
Oswald (5 Aug): *especially* 1 Peter 4.12–end; John 16.29–end
Perpetua, Felicity and comps (7 Mar): *especially* Revelation 12.10–12a; *also* Wisdom 3.1–7
Polycarp (23 Feb): *also* Revelation 2.8–11
Thomas Becket (29 Dec *or* 7 Jul): *especially* Matthew 10.28–33; *also* Ecclesiasticus 51.1–8
William Tyndale (6 Oct): *also* Proverbs 8.4–11; 2 Timothy 3.12–end

Teachers of the Faith and Spiritual Writers

I Kings 3.[6–10] 11–14; Proverbs 4.1–9; Wisdom 7.7–10, 15–16; Ecclesiasticus 39.1–10
Psalms 19.7–10; 34.11–17; 37.31–35; 119.89–96; 119.97–104
I Corinthians 1.18–25; *or* 2.1–10; *or* 2.9–end; Ephesians 3.8–12; 2 Timothy 4.1–8;
Titus 2.1–8
Matthew 5.13–19; *or* 13.52–end; *or* 23.8–12; Mark 4.1–9; John 16.12–15

Ambrose (7 Dec): *also* Isaiah 41.9*b*–13; Luke 22.24–30
Anselm (21 Apr): *also* Wisdom 9.13–end; Romans 5.8–11
Athanasius (2 May): *also* Ecclesiasticus 4.20–28; *also* Matthew 10.24–27
Augustine of Hippo (28 Aug): *especially* Ecclesiasticus 39.1–10; *also* Romans 13.11–13
Basil and Gregory (2 Jan): *especially* 2 Timothy 4.1–8; Matthew 5.13–19
Bernard (20 Aug): *especially* Revelation 19.5–9
Catherine of Siena (29 Apr): *also* Proverbs 8.1, 6–11; John 17.12–end
Francis de Sales (24 Jan): *also* Proverbs 3.13–18; John 3.17–21
Gregory the Great (3 Sept): *also* I Thessalonians 2.3–8
Gregory of Nyssa and Macrina (19 July): *especially* I Corinthians 2.9–13;
also Wisdom 9.13–17
Hilary (13 Jan): *also* I John 2.18–25; John 8.25–32
Irenaeus (28 June): *also* 2 Peter 1.16–end
Jeremy Taylor (13 Aug): *also* Titus 2.7–8, 11–14
John Bunyan (30 Aug): *also* Hebrews 12.1–2; Luke 21.21, 34–36
John Chrysostom (13 Sept): *especially* Matthew 5.13–19; *also* Jeremiah 1.4–10
John of the Cross (14 Dec): *especially* I Corinthians 2.1–10; *also* John 14.18–23
Leo (10 Nov): *also* I Peter 5.1–11
Richard Hooker (3 Nov): *especially* John 16.12–15; *also* Ecclesiasticus 44.10–15
Teresa of Avila (15 Oct): *also* Romans 8.22–27
Thomas Aquinas (28 Jan): *especially* Wisdom 7.7–10, 15–16; I Corinthians 2.9–end;
John 16.12–15
William Law (10 Apr): *especially* I Corinthians 2.9–end; *also* Matthew 17.1–9

Bishops and Other Pastors

I Samuel 16.1, 6–13; Isaiah 6.1–8; Jeremiah 1.4–10; Ezekiel 3.16–21; Malachi 2.5–7
Psalms 1; 15; 16.5–end; 96; 110
Acts 20.28–35; I Corinthians 4.1–5; 2 Corinthians 4.1–10 [or 1–2, 5–7];
    or 5.14–20; I Peter 5.1–4
Matthew 11.25–end; or 24.42–46; John 10.11–16; or 15.9–17; or 21.15–17

Augustine of Canterbury (26 May): also I Thessalonians 2.2b–8; Matthew 13.31–33
Charles Simeon (13 Nov): especially Malachi 2.5–7; also Colossians 1.3–8; Luke 8.4–8
David (1 Mar): also 2 Samuel 23.1–4; Psalm 89.19–22, 24
Dunstan (19 May): especially Matthew 24.42–46; also Exodus 31.1–5
Edward King (8 Mar): also Hebrews 13.1–8
George Herbert (27 Feb): especially Malachi 2.5–7; Matthew 11.25–end;
    also Revelation 19.5–9
Hugh (17 Nov); also I Timothy 6.11–16
John Keble (14 July): also Lamentations 3.19–26; Matthew 5.1–8
John and Charles Wesley (24 May): also Ephesians 5.15–20
Lancelot Andrewes (25 Sept): especially Isaiah 6.1–8
Martin of Tours (11 Nov): also I Thessalonians 5.1–11; Matthew 25.34–40
Nicholas (6 Dec): also Isaiah 61.1–3; I Timothy 6.6–11; Mark 10.13–16
Richard (16 June): also John 21.15–19
Swithun (15 July): also James 5.7–11, 13–18
Thomas Ken (8 June): especially 2 Corinthians 4.1–10 [or 1–2, 5–7]; Matthew 24.42–46
Wulfstan (19 Jan): especially Matthew 24.42–46

Members of Religious Communities

I Kings 19.9–18; Proverbs 10.27–end; Song of Solomon 8.6–7; Isaiah 61.10—62.5;
    Hosea 2.14–15, 19–20
Psalms 34.1–8; 112.1–9; 119.57–64; 123; 131
Acts 4.32–35; 2 Corinthians 10.17—11.2; Philippians 3.7–14; I John 2.15–17;
    Revelation 19.1, 5–9
Matthew 11.25–end; *or* 19.3–12; *or* 19.23–end; Luke 9.57–end; *or* 12.32–37

Aelred (12 Jan): *also* Ecclesiasticus 15.1–6
Alcuin (20 May): *also* Colossians 3.12–16; John 4.19–24
Antony (17 Jan): *especially* Philippians 3.7–14, *also* Matthew 19.16–26
Bede (25 May): *also* Ecclesiasticus 39.1–10
Benedict (11 July): *also* I Corinthians 3.10–11; Luke 18.18–22
Clare (11 Aug): *especially* Song of Solomon 8.6–7
Dominic (8 Aug): *also* Ecclesiasticus 39.1–10
Etheldreda (23 June): *also* Matthew 25.1–13
Francis of Assisi (4 Oct): *also* Galatians 6.14–end; Luke 12.22–34
Hilda (19 Nov): *especially* Isaiah 61.10—62.5
Hildegard (17 Sept): *also* I Corinthians 2.9–13; Luke 10.21–24
Julian of Norwich (8 May): *also* I Corinthians 13.8–end; Matthew 5.13–16
Vincent de Paul (27 Sept): *also* I Corinthians 1.25–end; Matthew 25.34–40

Missionaries

Isaiah 52.7–10; *or* 61.1–3a; Ezekiel 34.11–16; Jonah 3.1–5
Psalms 67; *or* 87; *or* 97; *or* 100; *or* 117
Acts 2.14, 22–36; *or* 13.46–49; *or* 16.6–10; *or* 26.19–23; Romans 15.17–21;
    2 Corinthians 5.11—6.2
Matthew 9.35–end; *or* 28.16–end; Mark 16.15–20; Luke 5.1–11; *or* 10.1–9

Aidan (31 Aug): *also* I Corinthians 9.16–19
Anskar (3 Feb): *especially* Isaiah 52.7–10; *also* Romans 10.11–15
Chad (2 Mar *or* 26 Oct): *also* I Timothy 6.11b–16
Columba (9 June): *also* Titus 2.11–end
Cuthbert (20 Mar *or* 4 Sept): *especially* Ezekiel 34.11–16; *also* Matthew 18.12–14
Cyril and Methodius (14 Feb): *especially* Isaiah 52.7–10; *also* Romans 10.11–15
Henry Martyn (19 Oct): *especially* Mark 16.15–end; *also* Isaiah 55.6–11
Ninian (16 Sept): *especially* Acts 13.46–49; Mark 16.15–end
Patrick (17 Mar): *also* Psalm 91.1–4, 13–end; Luke 10.1–12, 17–20
Paulinus (10 Oct); *especially* Matthew 28.16–end
Wilfrid (12 Oct): *especially* Luke 5.1–11; *also* I Corinthians 1.18–25
Willibrord (7 Nov): *especially* Isaiah 52.7–10; Matthew 28.16–end

Any Saint

General

Genesis 12.1–4; Proverbs 8.1–11; Micah 6.6–8; Ecclesiasticus 2.7–13 [14–end]
Psalms 32; 33.1–5; 119.1–8; 139.1–4 [5–12]; 145.8–14
Ephesians 3.14–19; *or* 6.11–18; Hebrews 13.7–8, 15–16; James 2.14–17;
    1 John 4.7–16; Revelation 21.[1–4] 5–7
Matthew 19.16–21; *or* 25.1–13; *or* 25.14–30; John 15.1–8; *or* 17.20–end

Christian rulers

1 Samuel 16.1–13*a*; 1 Kings 3.3–14
Psalms 72.1–7; 99
1 Timothy 2.1–6
Mark 10.42–45; Luke 14.27–33

Alfred the Great (26 Oct): *also* 2 Samuel 23.1–5; John 18.33–37
Edward the Confessor (13 Oct): *also* 2 Samuel 23.1–5; 1 John 4.13–16
Margaret of Scotland (16 Nov): *also* Proverbs 31.10–12, 20, 26–end;
    1 Corinthians 12.13—13.3; Matthew 25.34–end

Those working for the poor and underprivileged

Isaiah 58.6–11
Psalms 82; 146.5–10
Hebrews 13.1–3; 1 John 3.14–18
Matthew 5.1–12; *or* 25.31–end

Elizabeth of Hungary (18 Nov): *especially* Matthew 25.31–end; *also* Proverbs 31.10–end
Josephine Butler (30 May): *especially* Isaiah 58.6–11; *also* 1 John 3.18–23; Matthew 9.10–13
William Wilberforce, Olaudah Equiano and Thomas Clarkson (30 July): *also* Job 31.16–23;
    Galatians 3.26–end, 4.6–7; Luke 4.16–21

Men and women of learning

Proverbs 8.22–31; Ecclesiasticus 44.1–15
Psalms 36.5–10; 49.1–4
Philippians 4.7–8
Matthew 13.44–46, 52; John 7.14–18

Those whose holiness was revealed in marriage and family life

Proverbs 31.10–13, 19–20, 30–end; Tobit 8.4–7
Psalms 127; 128
1 Peter 3.1–9
Mark 3.31–end; Luke 10.38–end

Mary Sumner (9 Aug): *also* Hebrews 13.1–5
Monica (27 Aug): *also* Ecclesiasticus 26.1–3, 13–16

The Guidance of the Holy Spirit

Proverbs 24.3–7; Isaiah 30.15–21; Wisdom 9.13–17
Psalms 25.1–9; 104.26–33; 143.8–10
Acts 15.23–29; Romans 8:22–27; 1 Corinthians 12.4–13
Luke 14.27–33; John 14.23–26; *or* 16.13–15

Rogation Days
(15–17 May in 2023)

Deuteronomy 8.1–10; 1 Kings 8.35–40; Job 28.1–11
Psalms 104.21–30; 107.1–9; 121
Philippians 4.4–7; 2 Thessalonians 3.6–13; 1 John 5.12–15
Matthew 6.1–15; Mark 11.22–24; Luke 11.5–13

Harvest Thanksgiving

Year A	Year B	Year C
Deuteronomy 8.7–18 *or* 28.1–14	Joel 2.21–27	Deuteronomy 26.1–1
Psalm 65	Psalm 126	Psalm 100
2 Corinthians 9.6–end	1 Timothy 2.1–7; *or* 6.6–10	Philippians 4.4–9
Luke 12.16–30; *or* 17.11–19	Matthew 6.25–33	*or* Revelation 14.14–1
		John 6.25–35

Mission and Evangelism

Isaiah 49.1–6; *or* 52.7–10; Micah 4.1–5
Psalms 2; 46; 67
Acts 17.10–end; 2 Corinthians 5.14—6.2; Ephesians 2.13–end
Matthew 5.13–16; *or* 28.16–end; John 17.20–end

The Unity of the Church

Jeremiah 33.6–9*a*; Ezekiel 36.23–28; Zephaniah 3.16–end
Psalms 100; 122; 133
Ephesians 4.1–6; Colossians 3.9–17; 1 John 4.9–15
Matthew 18.19–22; John 11.45–52; *or* 17.11*b*–23

The Peace of the World

Isaiah 9.1–6; *or* 57.15–19; Micah 4.1–5
Psalms 40.14–17; 72.1–7; 85.8–13
Philippians 4.6–9; 1 Timothy 2.1–6; James 3.13–18
Matthew 5.43–end; John 14.23–29; *or* 15.9–17

Social Justice and Responsibility

Isaiah 32.15–end; Amos 5.21–24; or 8.4–7; Acts 5.1–11
Psalms 31.21–24; 85.1–7; 146.5–10
Colossians 3.12–15; James 2.1–4
Matthew 5.1–12; or 25.31–end; Luke 16.19–end

Ministry, including Ember Days
(See page 7)

Numbers 11.16–17, 24–29; or 27.15–end; 1 Samuel 16.1–13a; Isaiah 6.1–8;
    or 61.1–3; Jeremiah 1.4–10
Psalms 40.8–13; 84.8–12; 89.19–25; 101.1–5, 7; 122
Acts 20.28–35; 1 Corinthians 3.3–11; Ephesians 4.4–16; Philippians 3.7–14
Luke 4.16–21; or 12.35–43; or 22.24–27; John 4.31–38; or 15.5–17

In Time of Trouble

Genesis 9.8–17; Job 1.13–end; Isaiah 38.6–11
Psalms 86.1–7; 107.4–15; 142.1–7
Romans 3.21–26; Romans 8.18–25; 2 Corinthians 8.1–5, 9
Mark 4.35–end; Luke 12.1–7; John 16.31–end

For the Sovereign

Joshua 1.1–9; Proverbs 8.1–16
Psalms 20; 101; 121
Romans 13.1–10; Revelation 21.22—22.4
Matthew 22.16–22; Luke 22.24–30

The anniversary of HM The Queen's accession is 6 February.

The following provision may be used for a monthly cycle of psalmody in place of the psalms provided in the tables in this booklet. It is based on the provision in The Book of Common Prayer.

	Morning Prayer	**Evening Prayer**
1	1—5	6—8
2	9—11	12—14
3	15—17	18
4	19—21	22—23
5	24—26	27—29
6	30—31	32—34
7	35—36	37
8	38—40	41—43
9	44—46	47—49
10	50—52	53—55
11	56—58	59—61
12	62—64	65—67
13	68	69—70
14	71—72	73—74
15	75—77	78
16	79—81	82—85
17	86—88	89
18	90—92	93—94
19	95—97	98—101
20	102—103	104
21	105	106
22	107	108—109
23	110—112	113—115
24	116—118	119.1–32
25	119.33–72	119.73–96
26	119.97–144	119.145–176
27	120—125	126—131
28	132—135	136—138
29	139—140	141—143
30	144—146	147—150

In February the psalms are read only to the 28th or 29th day of the month.

In January, March, May, July, August, October and December, all of which have 31 days, the same psalms are read on the last day of the month (being an ordinary weekday) which were read the day before, or else the psalms of the monthly course omitted on one of the Sundays in that month.